THE PONT DU GARD

'One of the most daring and beautiful constructions by Roman engineers and architects.' This mighty bridge, rising 160 ft. above the river bed, was part of the water-supply system for the Roman town of Nemansus (near Nîmes). The water flowed in a channel on the topmost row of arches.

EVERYDAY LIFE
IN ROME

IN THE TIME OF CAESAR
AND CICERO

by

H. A. TREBLE, M.A.

and

K. M. KING, B.A.

Assistant Masters
Selhurst Grammar School
Croydon

OXFORD
AT THE CLARENDON PRESS

Oxford University Press, Ely House, London W.1

GLASGOW NEW YORK TORONTO MELBOURNE WELLINGTON
CAPE TOWN IBADAN NAIROBI DAR ES SALAAM LUSAKA ADDIS ABABA
DELHI BOMBAY CALCUTTA MADRAS KARACHI LAHORE DACCA
KUALA LUMPUR SINGAPORE HONG KONG TOKYO

FIRST PUBLISHED 1930
REPRINTED 1931, 1932, 1935, 1939, 1945, 1947,
1949, 1951, 1953, 1958, 1964, 1966, 1967, 1969,
1970, 1972

PRINTED IN GREAT BRITAIN

PREFACE

THIS little book on Roman life is intended in the first place for young pupils beginning the study of Latin. They will doubtless be attracted more by the illustrations than by the text; but as the text is largely a translation of the illustrations into language simple enough to be understood by youthful minds, it is hoped that even a preliminary reading will be found to make an instructive beginning and to do something towards creating an intelligent interest which can gradually develop into real knowledge. A second and more intensive study of the book, it is suggested, can profitably be made in the year of the School Leaving Examination when the Latin terms, largely neglected during the first-year reading, can really be assimilated.

The style of the book has been left as simple as possible and all unnecessary detail has been avoided. At the same time we believe that the facts given are in every respect in line with the most recent researches of modern archaeology.

Our warmest thanks are due to Dr. E. Norman Gardiner, who has shown the keenest interest in the book throughout its preparation and who has placed at our disposal the benefits of his ripe scholarship and practical experience; and to the officers of the Clarendon Press for the choice of illustrations.

Three books have been largely used for reference. First, there is W. Warde Fowler's brilliant and absorbing study of *Social Life at Rome in the Age of Cicero*; secondly, for all technical matters, H. Stuart Jones's *Companion to Roman History*; thirdly, for illustrations from Latin literature, *The Life of Rome*, compiled by Messrs. Rogers and Harley.

CROYDON,   H. A. T.
December 1929.   K. M. K.

PUBLISHER'S NOTE
ON TWELFTH IMPRESSION

In this impression opportunity has been taken to modernize the text in a few places, the most important of which is the account of the coinage on pp. 84-85. The publishers are grateful to Mr. M. W. Frederiksen, Fellow of Worcester College, for his help in this.

July 1966

CONTENTS

LIST OF ILLUSTRATIONS

LIST OF ILLUSTRATIONS

COVER: The Forum, Rome. *Photograph, J. Allan Cash*

The Foundation of Rome. A typical Italian hill town

I

A BRIEF SKETCH OF ROMAN HISTORY

THE beginnings of Roman history are hidden by picturesque but untrustworthy legends, in which, however, we can discover certain broad facts concerning the origins of the Roman people. The Romans first appear in true history as one of several tribes settled in the middle of the Italian peninsula. We do not know where they came from in the first instance; but they took up their abode just where the Apennine mountains sweep nearest to the east coast, leaving a fairly wide plain on their western side. Through this plain flows the Tiber in an almost north-south direction; it is the only river of any real importance south of the Apennines.

The plain on the south-eastern side of the Tiber was known as Latium, and tradition tells us that here, some twenty miles from the sea, the City of Rome was built in 753 B.C. The earliest settlement had been on the Alban Mount, away from the river, but was transferred later to a second site, farther north, which could be more easily defended against the most dangerous of Rome's neighbours. These were the Etruscans, who had come into Italy later than the Romans and had settled in the region now known as Tuscany. Rome was built on the southern bank of the Tiber, where a group of low hills, rising fairly steeply from the river, formed a valuable means of defence.

There were other alien settlers farther south—the Greeks, who had founded colonies round the southern shores of Italy. In the early days, however, the Romans did not need to trouble greatly about the Greeks, since they were separated from them by hardy mountain tribes of similar race to themselves. These were the Samnites, whose country lay to the south-east of Latium. Yet another group of tribes of similar race, the Umbrians, were settled in the mountains to the

north-east. Thus, at the outset of her history as we know it, Rome was one of a number of small cities in the plain of Latium, with tribes of the same race in the mountains to the east and a dangerous, restless enemy to the north.

In spite of her defensive position, it would appear that at some time in the sixth century B.C. the Etruscans succeeded in capturing Rome, but the conquerors were driven out by a rebellion of the Roman nobles in 509 B.C. Tarquin the Proud, the king who was expelled, tried to regain the throne with the help of Etruscan armies, but without success.

The Romans hated the very name of king and they now set up a republic. The city was governed by two consuls, elected to hold office for one year. This was too short a period for them to become tyrannical; moreover, one consul could always act as a check on the other. This arrangement lasted till the Empire was founded by Augustus nearly five centuries later. (Five hundred years ago from now, the Wars of the Roses were still being fought. When we think how many changes there have been in the government of England since then, it is evident that the Romans chose for themselves a form of government that stood the test of time remarkably well. In this respect they showed at a very early date one of their greatest characteristics.)

At the beginning of the Republic, Rome was only one of the cities of Latium, and, though the most outstanding of them, she was not very much more powerful than the rest. This can be seen from the treaties that were made between the various Latin cities, by which each had the right of trade and intermarriage with the people of all the other cities in the league, including Rome. Now it always happens sooner or later in every group of individuals, or of cities, or of nations, that one becomes more powerful than the rest. Very soon it was clear that Rome would be the chief city in the Latin league. When the others saw this they were jealous, and actually gave no help when Rome was nearly overwhelmed by the Gauls from Northern Italy in 390 B.C.

But Rome weathered the storm, and coming out of her

danger stronger than before, she altered her treaties with the
Latin cities so that, while each might trade and intermarry
only with the Romans, Rome had the advantage of both
trading and intermarrying with the citizens of all the other
cities. In this way the Latins were the first to pay the penalty
of standing against Rome. At the same time Rome made
an alliance with the great African city of Carthage, which
promised to help in keeping Rome at the head of the league.
Rome strengthened her hold on Latium by building the first
of her great military roads (the *Via Latina*) and founding
fortresses (*coloniae*) at points of military importance.

The extension of her power over the whole of Latium
brought Rome into conflict with the hardy mountaineers of
Samnium. They proved to be formidable enemies, and
Rome suffered one of her greatest humiliations when a whole
army surrendered at a place known as the Caudine Forks in
the course of the Samnite Wars. But in the end Rome pre-
vailed, in spite of a combined movement against her by the
Samnites, the Umbrians, and the Etruscans. Her victory was
due to the advantages of her geographical position and the
fine character of her citizens.

The war with Samnium brought Rome to the borders of
the Greek lands in the south—Magna Graecia, as that part of
Italy was called. The leading city was Tarentum; and it was
clear that against this city Rome would soon have to pit her
strength. The Greeks sought an ally in Pyrrhus, king of
Epirus in north-western Greece, a king who dreamed of
rivalling the conquests of Alexander the Great. It is true
that he won several battles at the expense of the Romans, but
at such a cost that he was obliged to return to Greece and
leave the Greek colonies to fall into the hands of Rome.
Thus, by the year 270 B.C., Rome was mistress of all Italy
south of the Apennines, though we must note that she had

An Etruscan nobleman and his wife. A terra-cotta sculpture from an
Etruscan tomb

A group of bronze figures of the sixth century B.C., representing an
Etruscan peasant ploughing. Behind him stands a figure of the
goddess Minerva

THE ETRUSCANS

made no attempt to spread her power over the valley of the Po, between the Apennines and the Alps.

Rome was now well on the road of conquest and could not draw back. Before long a struggle began between Rome and Carthage. This great trading city on the north coast of Africa

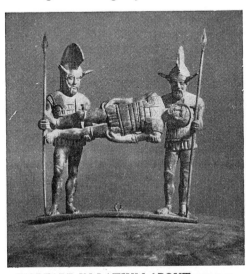

WARFARE IN LATIUM ABOUT 350 B.C.
An early bronze group found at Palestrina, showing two bearded warriors carrying the dead body of a comrade

was the most dangerous rival that Rome ever had, and the war was a struggle for existence between the two cities. Several times it seemed that Rome would be defeated, but the patriotism of her citizens saved her again and again. At last, in 146 B.C., Carthage was finally destroyed. Rome was now mistress of the western Mediterranean, and had the beginnings of an overseas empire. Her wealth and power were increasing rapidly. Before long all the Mediterranean lands were under her rule.

These successes of Rome brought various difficulties and problems with them. Victorious generals led home in triumph thousands of slaves who did the work that the citizens had done before. The rich became richer while the poor became poorer. Then two brothers belonging to one of the noblest

JULIUS CAESAR

families, Tiberius and Gaius Gracchus, tried to put matters right. Tiberius wanted to have the lands belonging to the State divided more fairly among the poor citizens. But there were many who opposed the plan, and Tiberius, who set the laws aside in order to have his way, was killed in a riot that his enemies had brought about (133 B.C.). Nine years later Gaius tried more vigorously to carry on his brother's work, but before long he met a similar fate.

These unruly years gave the army a chance to gain power. Often a successful general—that is, one who could reward his men with much plunder—had more power in the Roman world than the consuls had, though sometimes generals used their power to have themselves elected to the consulate. Marius and the still more powerful Sulla were the first of these great generals.

Their fame has been overshadowed by the greater fame of two generals that came after them—Pompey and Julius Caesar. Pompey had great success in his wars in the East, and for some time was the greatest man in the Roman world. At this period Caesar was making a name for himself in Gaul, i.e. modern France. Soon it became clear that neither Pompey nor Caesar would be content with second place. Civil war broke out. Pompey was defeated at Pharsalia in Greece, and was murdered soon afterwards in Egypt.

Julius Caesar was now a king in all but name. He used his power wisely and so much for the benefit of the people that he was offered the crown, though Rome had been a republic for more than four centuries. He refused to accept the crown; but there were some in Rome, including his friend Brutus, who feared his power. Rather than see him king they hatched a plot against him, and on 15 March 44 B.C. Caesar was murdered in the Senate House.

The conspirators did not long remain in Rome, and soon an army was led against them to avenge the death of Caesar. Its leaders, who were called the Triumvirs, were Octavius (Caesar's nephew and heir), Mark Antony, and Lepidus. At Philippi in Greece the army of the conspirators was defeated. The Triumvirs now had all the power in their hands, but before long they quarrelled. Lepidus, the least important, soon ceased to count. Antony stayed idling in Egypt at the court of Queen Cleopatra, while Augustus (who had taken his uncle's name, Caesar) made ready a fleet. With this he utterly defeated Antony at Actium in 31 B.C. Antony killed himself rather than fall into his rival's hands, and Augustus Caesar became master of the Roman world.

For some years he carried on the pretence that there was no change of government, but in 27 B.C., when he was consul for the seventh time, he took the title of *Princeps*. This marked the end of the Republic and the beginning of the Empire.

Rome had not quite reached the limits of her territorial power; but the civil strife of the preceding century had weakened the moral strength of the Romans, and already the seeds of decay had been sown. There were still great conquests to be achieved, and great additions to be made to Latin literature and art, but the old virtues of self-restraint (*continentia*), steadfastness (*constantia*), and manliness (*virtus*) had almost vanished from the Roman character.

II

THE CITY OF ROME

IN the last chapter we touched briefly upon the geographical advantages of Rome. These consisted of the hills, the river Tiber, and the broad plain of Latium across which a system of military roads was constructed. The earliest settlement was on the Palatine, but the later City included a number of other hills. They were the Quirinal, Viminal, Esquiline, and Caelian Hills, all spurs of the table-land abutting on the river; the isolated Janiculum on the western side of the Tiber; and the lesser Pincian and Aventine Hills to the north and south of the main group. The valleys between these hills were swampy and often flooded in spite of the great drainage sewers (*cloacae*) that emptied into the river.

The Tiber, which formed the chief defence against Etruscan attacks, was a swift and turbulent stream, discoloured with the mud that it carried down from the mountains. This mud formed dangerous shoals at the river-mouth and for a long time prevented Ostia from becoming as important as the more distant Puteoli, the chief port of Rome. The Tiber

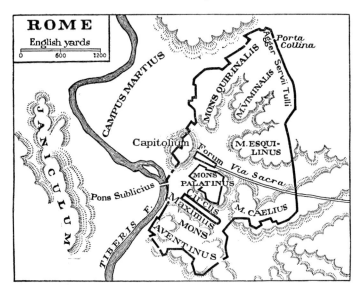

gave easy access to the mountains of the interior on the one side and to the coast on the other; yet Rome was far enough from the estuary to be safe from attacks from the sea. When the network of military roads was complete (the *Via Latina*, *Appia*, *Flaminia*, and others less important) the strategic position of Rome was unrivalled in the whole of Italy.

In order to get some idea of the City of Rome, let us go back in imagination to Caesar's day and walk through the ancient streets filled with the crowds and noisy with the bustle of the metropolis of the world. At that time the population was about half a million—many times greater than that of the earliest days.

It may well be supposed that the wall built by Servius Tullius, the sixth king of Rome (578–535 B.C.), embraced a good deal of open space where refugees from outside might encamp with their possessions in time of war. When wars broke out, the country-folk would come in with

> . . . droves of mules and asses,
>   Laden with skins of wine,
> And endless flocks of sheep and goats,
>   And endless herds of kine,
> And endless trains of wagons
>   That creaked beneath the weight
> Of corn-sacks and of household goods.

But by the first century B.C. all the space inside the wall was filled up and already buildings were being erected outside. The working classes were crowded together in great tenement blocks, for only the wealthiest could afford separate houses. Space was valuable, and the streets were often mere alleys, so Julius Caesar made a law that no vehicles should use the streets in the day-time. We can picture ancient Rome an overcrowded city of narrow lanes with overhanging houses, not unlike the oldest parts of London.

We will begin our imaginary tour from the Janiculum Hill on the right bank of the Tiber. Here was the earliest fortress, to guard the city from possible attacks by the Etruscans from the north. The road we follow runs down the slope towards the Pons Aemilius by which we cross the Tiber. On our left, upstream, we can see a ship-like island in the river, on which stands the earliest hospital in Rome, dedicated to Aesculapius, the god of healing. To the right is the open mouth of the Cloaca Maxima, the main sewer which drains away the water from the low-lying parts of the city. Beside it is the ancient wooden bridge, the Pons Sublicius, which Ancus Martius built. When Lars Porsena came with his Etruscan armies in 508 B.C. to help Tarquin the Proud to regain the throne, the Janiculum was taken by storm, as Macaulay tells in *The Lay of Horatius*. Straight towards the Pons Sublicius swept down the Etruscans, and only by the felling of the bridge could the city be saved. Then Horatius with two companions, Lartius and Herminius, guarded the bridge while the citizens hewed down its piles with axes. Just as the bridge fell, Lartius and Herminius leapt back to safety, but Horatius stayed too long. It seemed that he must perish; but, having commended his life to Father Tiber, he plunged into the muddy yellow river, and swam ashore.

We leave the bridges behind us and enter the city, noticing the splendid buildings on the Palatine Hill in front. We first reach the Forum Boarium, the cattle market, where we are reminded that the earliest Romans were workers on the soil. From the market-place we turn to the left along the once marshy hollow of Velabrum, leading directly to the Forum Romanum, at the foot of the Capitoline Hill. Long since this Forum has ceased to be what its name suggests—a market-place; it is now the centre of the city's life, where bankers and money-lenders have taken the place of shopkeepers.

In the Forum we can realize that we are in the heart of the chief city in the world. All around us rise famous structures with the very history of Rome built into their walls. There, on the north-west side, is the Temple of Concord, begun in 367 B.C. to mark the end of the struggle between Patricians and Plebeians. Above it is the Tabularium,[1] where all the public records are kept; and on the south side the Temple

---

[1] The lower parts of this building still exist.

of Saturn, where the treasure of the city is stored. Not far away, and facing down the Via Sacra, is the Rostra. This is a public platform, whence orators address the crowd, and it takes its name from the beaks of ships with which it is adorned. These had been captured by Maenius in the Latin

A ship-like island in the river
The *Isola Tiberina* in the middle of the Tiber

Wars and they remained as a lasting trophy of the early struggles of Rome. (In our day it has become the custom to commemorate our victories with captured guns.)

Formerly, till Julius Caesar moved them, the Rostra stood on the north-eastern side of the Forum below the Comitium. In the very early days of the city this was marked out and reserved as a consecrated place of assembly for the citizens. Hard by, on the north side of the Forum, is the Curia where the Senate meets.

On other sides of the Forum there are great halls, called *basilicae*, in which various kinds of public business are transacted. They are simply roofed halls divided into aisles by rows of columns. At one end there is a raised platform from which the magistrate administers justice. They serve as courts of justice, exchanges for merchants, and places of meeting for the people at large.

The oldest basilica in the Forum is the Basilica Porcia, built by Cato in 184 B.C., on the western side of the Comitium. On the north side of the Forum stands the Basilica Aemilia, which has been rebuilt in Julius Caesar's time. But the greatest of the three is the Basilica Julia on the south side of the Forum, adjoining the Temple of Saturn. This was known at one time as the Basilica Sempronia, but as Julius Caesar began its rebuilding on a larger scale, it now bears his name. We approach its stately portico by a flight of steps leading from the level of the Forum, and enter a magnificent central hall. It is paved with multicoloured marble, and an arcade of pillars bears a gallery with windows above. At the far end we can see a series of compartments (*tabernae*) used for business purposes. These are the chief *basilicae* at the end of this first century B.C., but in the Imperial age there will be several other and greater ones built to meet the growing needs of public business.

The Forum we see is not yet adorned with the columns, statues, and triumphal arches which later Emperors will set up. Round about us there are seething crowds who jostle their way noisily as they go about their business or wait idly for something to happen—a speech from the Rostra, the opening of a trial in the law-courts near by, or a religious procession down the Sacred Way.

We will leave behind us the crowds of the Forum and climb the Capitoline Hill. At the northern end is the citadel which

IN THE FORUM

The ruins of the Basilica Julia as they are to-day. The tall building in the background is the Palazzo Senatorio, built on the site of the Tabularium. The tall pillars in front are the ruins of the Temple of Saturn

held out so stubbornly against the Gauls in 390 B.C. The besiegers tried one night to take the fort by surprise after climbing the cliff-like hill under cover of darkness; but the sacred geese, kept there for sacrifices, gave the alarm in time and the attack failed. At the other end of the summit of this hill is the great Temple of Jupiter, chief of the gods, who is worshipped here together with Juno and Minerva. It is the largest temple in Rome.

Outside, to the south, the hill descends by a steep cliff known as the Tarpeian Rock (see p. 149). The name commemorates the fate of the unhappy Vestal, Tarpeia, who betrayed the citadel to the Sabines in the legendary days of Rome. It is said that Tarpeia met the Sabine captain, Titus Tatius, at the fountain where she went at sunset to draw water, and that she coveted the gold bracelet on the warrior's arm. He gave it to her, and promised that she should have all that his men wore on their left arms if she would open the gates of the fortress to them. She consented, but when she let in the enemy that night, Tatius struck her down with the shield that he bore on his left arm, and, in fulfilment of his promise, as his men passed in they threw down their shields on the traitor's body. Having taken the fortress, the Sabines buried Tarpeia under the rock that bears her name.

From the Capitoline Hill we look out north-westwards beyond the walls to the Campus Martius, the great open space in a bend of the Tiber, used for military exercises. This 'Field of Mars' was once public land, and it reminds us of the open spaces adjoining the later cities of London and Paris; in the one we find St. Martin's Fields, in the other the Champs-Élysées. In the two modern cities the open spaces have long vanished; and as we look out on the Campus Martius we can see that already buildings are encroaching upon it. The largest that we see is the Circus

Flaminius, which has stood there since the end of the wars with Carthage. There is also Pompey's Theatre, and later on there will be other great public buildings—the Baths of

A triumphal arch set up in Rome by the Emperor Titus. The Marble Arch in London is an imitation of the Roman type

Nero and Agrippa, and the Pantheon, a burial-place for the Emperors.

We now make our way back to the Forum and thence down the uneven, crooked Via Sacra, lined with the oldest and most honoured temples in Rome. On our right we pass first the Temple of Castor, and then the spring of Juturna. Macaulay has told how the twin-brother gods, Castor and

Pollux, fought for the Romans in the battle of Lake Regillus against the Latins: then, when the victory was won,

> On rode they to the Forum,
>> While laurel-boughs and flowers,
> From house-tops and from windows
>> Fell on their crests in showers.
> When they drew nigh to Vesta,
>> They vaulted down amain,
> And washed their horses in the well
>> That springs by Vesta's fane.

Leaving the Temple of Castor and this spring that is still held in reverence, we reach the Temple of Vesta and the house where her priestesses, the Vestal Virgins, live together as in a convent. These virgins tend the never-dying fire which symbolizes the life of the city. Opposite the temple and in the middle of the Sacred Way stands the Regia, once the royal palace but now the residence of the Pontifex Maximus. Other temples will be crowded into this short street of less than half a mile which is indeed the holiest ground in Rome.

We reach the eastern end of the Sacred Way and turn to the right. Before continuing we can obtain a general view of the Quirinal, Esquiline, and Caelian Hills that sweep in a semicircle round the eastern side of the city: while just before us is the place where the huge Flavian Amphitheatre (better known as the Colosseum) will be built.

All this time, as we walk, we have had the Palatine Hill on our right. This was the site of the first settlement from which the city grew, and here are many relics, including the hut of Romulus, which is connected with the early legendary days. In the course of time this hill has become the most fashionable quarter of the city, and here the Emperors will build their palaces.

We now proceed along the hollow between the Palatine

and Caelian Hills, till we reach the Porta Capena. Here the Appian Way leaves the city, cleaving its straight route right through the countryside to the hilly district of Samnium which defied Rome so long. Along this straight, tree-bordered road we can see the tombs of famous Romans.

The *Via Sacra* leading up to the Capitol

But we shall not go outside the city yet. Let us turn our steps back instead to the huge building on our left, the Circus Maximus. It stands between the Palatine and Aventine Hills. Here chariot-races take place for the amusement of the idle mob in the city who cannot or will not work. As we turn the eastern corner of the Circus, at the foot of the Aventine, we see before us, on the right, the cattle market where we started our walk.

In such a tour as that sketched out above, the oldest and most famous parts of Rome would have been visited, but little would be seen of those parts of the city where the ordinary people dwell. Like those of modern London, the inhabitants of ancient Rome lived on the outskirts away from the busy heart of the city. The residential quarters were on certain of the hills. The patricians lived on the Palatine; wealthy plebeians had splendid mansions on the Quirinal. On the other hills, the Esquiline, Caelian, and Aventine, which formed a semicircular border round the middle of the city, the working classes had their dwellings. The poorest were to be found in the unhealthy hollows between the hills. In these districts were very large tenement-buildings, called *insulae* because they were whole blocks surrounded by streets as 'islands' are surrounded by water. These tenements were usually of three or four storeys, the ground floor being occupied by shops (*tabernae*) with open fronts to the street, and in these many families were herded together in great discomfort. They were often rickety tumble-down buildings, the upper parts of wood, top-heavy and liable to collapse. They were usually in disrepair and often on fire.

III

ROMAN HOUSES IN TOWN AND COUNTRY

It was said of Augustus Caesar that he found Rome made of brick and rebuilt it in marble. Though this statement may have something of exaggeration, it is none the less true that Rome grew up in a somewhat haphazard fashion and not according to any particular plan. We have seen already that the majority of the ordinary people lived in great tenement

EXCAVATIONS IN PROGRESS AT POMPEII

Part of the street of the Roman town has been laid bare, and digging is going on at the end, where the present level of the surrounding earth can be seen, about 18 ft. above the street level

buildings and that only the fairly well-to-do had houses of their own. By the first century B.C., Greek influences had brought many changes in the plan and arrangement of Roman

A burial urn made in the form of a one-roomed wooden hut. This urn (made of brown earthenware) was found in a prehistoric cemetery at Rome

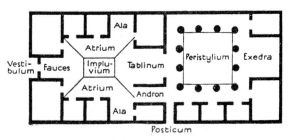

A typical Pompeian house

houses, so that they were very different from the houses of an earlier day. Our knowledge is derived from the ruins that have been dug out at Pompeii and Ostia, and also on the Palatine Hill in Rome.

These show us the latest forms of the houses of the wealthy, but the earlier houses were much simpler. The simplest was just a one-roomed hut, with a hole in the middle of the roof to let out smoke and admit light. We know pretty well what these early houses looked like because burial urns were made like them and some of these have been found.

As the Romans became wealthier and more civilized they had better houses. But they still kept the idea of the hut with a hole in the roof, for the next type of house was merely an elaboration of the primitive hut. There was one chief room, the *atrium*, round which were grouped a few small and comparatively unimportant apartments. The *atrium* was so called because its rafters were black (*ater*) with smoke from the family fire that was lighted there. The life of the family, in all its different aspects, was centred in the *atrium*. It was the living-room, where the work (such as spinning and weaving) was done, and where the family ate their meals. The master of the house kept his money-chest there, fastened to the floor. Here, too, were the Penates, the gods that guarded the material goods of the house, and the Lararium, the shrine of the family gods. But perhaps the most striking feature of the *atrium* was the square hole in the middle of the roof, which sloped inwards so that rain-water drained into a tank in the floor below: this was simply a survival from the hut of early times. Beyond the *atrium* at the back of the house there was a small garden; and sometimes a small open shop (*taberna*) would be found on each side of the street-entrance. At Pompeii the so-called House of the Surgeon gives a good example of a typical Roman house.

When Greek ideas were copied in Rome, houses became larger and more elaborate. The most important change was the addition of a whole new section, comprising an open courtyard (*peristylium*), bordered on two or more sides with columns, and surrounded with additional rooms. The *peri-*

stylium and the adjoining rooms came to be the private part
of the house. Meals were eaten in the *tablinum* that lay
between the *atrium* and the newer parts, and the family gods
and shrines were moved out of the *atrium*, which was now
used as the chief reception-room, while the *peristylium* with

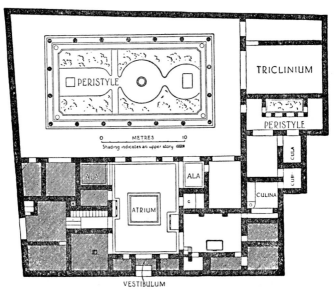

Ground-plan of the House of the Vettii

its adjoining apartments was reserved for private and family
use. We may note in passing that the new portions bore the
Greek name *peristylium*, while the original rooms had Latin
names (e.g. *atrium*, *tablinum*, *ala*).

Since the Roman houses were as varied in type as those of
to-day, it is difficult to find and describe a standard form of
Roman house. We shall gain a clearer impression of a typical
house by reconstructing in imagination one of the Pompeian
houses that have been dug out from the volcanic ash and lava

that buried them during the great eruption of Vesuvius in
A.D. 79. At Pompeii, it is true, Greek influences were very
strong; but the town was a favourite resort of wealthy
Romans, and no doubt their houses at Rome were similar to
those at Pompeii.

Let us visit the house of the Vettii, a wealthy family owning
many vineyards in the neighbourhood and having large
interests in the wine trade. The house is not particularly
large, but it owes its fame to the series of wall-paintings with
which it is adorned. It stands in a quiet part of Pompeii,
approached by a rather narrow cobbled street. The bareness
of the outer wall gives no hint of the magnificent interior.
The rooms are mostly lighted from the inside, but some
houses opening on the main streets had spacious balconies
and large windows on the first floor.

We step from the street into a lofty entrance-porch. Before
us is a massive pair of heavy folding-doors, but these are
opened only in the morning when the crowd of visitors and
clients is collecting. We will enter by a smaller side-door and
pass through a lobby into the principal *atrium* (for this house
is rather unusual in having two *atria*, as we shall see).

This first *atrium* is a magnificent reception-room, having
a floor of mosaic, and containing several fine wall-paintings.
It is extremely lofty. In summer it is shady and cool, but
in winter it is less pleasant since there are no means of heating
it except by braziers of charcoal. There is very little furniture
in the *atrium*—simply a few carved benches and a ceremonial
bed to remind us that the *atrium* was at one time the chief
living-room. Curtains divide the small side-rooms from the
main apartment. The massive beams of the ceiling slope
downwards towards the middle to the large square opening
that supplies the light. Below the opening there is a tank

sunk in the floor to catch the rain-water from the roof. Against the wall on each side of this tank there is a finely carved money-chest on a pedestal.

Passing through the *atrium* we reach the spacious outer courtyard. There is a covered verandah, supported on columns, round all four sides of the courtyard—a pleasant garden-plot, bright with flowers and shrubs, adorned with marble busts on pillars, and furnished with four round marble tables. At each corner and in the middle of the sides there is the tinkling sound of water falling from fountains into marble basins. Some of the fountains are of marble, but two are of bronze in the shape of a boy holding a duck from whose beak the water flows.

Let us now cross the courtyard to the main dining-room at the opposite corner. It is one of the most famous rooms in Pompeii on account of its wall-paintings. The owners of the house are not ashamed of the trade that has given them their wealth, and the most interesting pictures in this room are those showing Cupids busy with all kinds of trade and ordinary labour such as gardening, selling flowers, pressing olives for oil, goldsmiths' work, and wine-selling.

Leaving this beautiful room we pass into the main court-yard once more in order to reach the smaller garden-court that opens from it. This is obviously the one used only by the family, for there are bedrooms and a smaller dining-room adjoining it.

There are still the rooms opening from the main *atrium* for us to visit. The domestic quarters are all grouped in the north-east front corner of the house round a second small *atrium*. This is of the usual type and devoted to family use. Here we find the *lararium*, the shrine of the household gods. This also is beautifully painted. The picture shows the genius

The inner courtyard (*peristylium*) of the House of the Vettii at Pompeii. Against the second column from the left, in the photograph, can be seen one of the bronze fountains of a boy holding a duck

of the master of the house holding the box of incense and the libation dish with which the religious ceremonies of the household are carried out. On each side of him is the figure of a Lar (household god), in an attitude of dancing, and holding a drinking-horn. Below the figures is the serpent that is depicted on all such altars. See illustration, p. 39.

One of the wall-paintings in the *triclinium* of the House of the Vettii, representing cupids as wine-sellers. On the left is a customer, to whom the wine-merchant is handing a sample of wine

Crossing the chief *atrium* once more, we find on the southern side a corridor that leads to a door in a side-street, and also to the staircase that takes us to several small rooms forming a second storey along the whole front of the house. These would be used for various private purposes, sometimes as extra dining-rooms, sometimes as store-rooms, and one of them, perhaps, as a schoolroom.

The houses at Ostia may have been more typically Roman. At Pompeii there was plenty of space for building, so houses could be spread out over a large area rather than built upwards to a great height. But at Ostia, as at Rome, the amount of space for building was limited, and so it became the practice to build houses of several storeys, adding to the accommodation by increasing the height but not the area of the building.

Rome was a noisy bustling place and unhealthy in the summer months; so it became the fashion for rich men to

THE PAINTED ALTAR OF THE HOUSEHOLD GODS

have country houses within easy reach of the city. For instance, Cicero, though not very well-to-do, at one time had six country houses in various places near Rome. They were luxurious and beautiful mansions, as we can tell from pictures of them that still exist and from the detailed descriptions to be found in the letters of Cicero and other writings. These country houses often served as convenient stopping-places when a rich man was travelling. He would arrange the stages of his journey so as to spend the night at a friend's house, though for ordinary travellers there were taverns like those that have been brought to light at Ostia and Pompeii.

Though such country houses (known as *villae urbanae*) were largely modelled, as their name suggests, on the town houses of the rich, there was one noticeable difference between the two. The *peristylium* was the most important part of the country house, as all the pictures show. Sometimes, indeed, there was no *atrium* at all; and even if there were it was usually behind the garden court and kept for private use.

In addition to the rooms found in a town house, there were many others added to a *villa urbana* to suit the tastes of the owner. There would be a picture gallery in some houses; in others a library, like that of Lucullus, where Cicero used to study when staying at one of his villas near by. There would be hot-air baths, and sometimes a swimming-tank. Outside there were gardens, arbours, and fish-ponds; and colonnades to relieve the flatness of the blank outside walls. Usually the villas were built in positions commanding fine views, for the Romans as a whole had a great love for the beauties of nature.

Besides the country houses of wealthy city men, there were the farmsteads known as *villae rusticae*. One of the best known is that at Boscoreale, near Pompeii, which consisted of a house of the usual kind together with the farm buildings a little distance away. As the plan shows, these covered a rectangular space, with a large threshing-floor, paved with pounded tiles, projecting at the south-eastern end. Practically in the middle, on the western side was an entrance courtyard, surrounded by a colonnade that supported an upper storey. This courtyard gave access to the various buildings. At the

A ROMAN HOUSE AT OSTIA

An imaginary restoration, based on the ruins existing there to-day. It is a four-storeyed tenement-house, the ground floor occupied by shops, the upper floors by private flats

north-western end, occupying about a quarter of the whole, there were the living-rooms—a kitchen and a bakehouse; a dining-room; bedrooms and bathrooms; and a tool-house. The rest of the space was taken up with buildings needed for the work of the farm. A good deal of room was needed for the various processes connected with the making of wine. Two large wine-presses adjoined the courtyard, and from these the

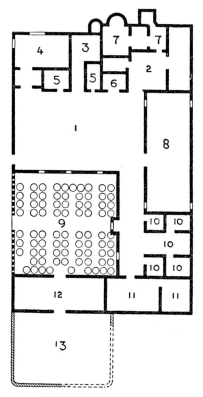

KEY

1. Entrance courtyard
2. Kitchen
3. Bakehouse
4. Dining-room
5. Bedrooms
6. Tool-house
7. Bathrooms
8. Wine-presses
9. Fermentation shed, filled with open wine vats
10. Slaves' quarters
11. Olive presses and store-rooms for oil
12. Wagon-shed
13. Threshing-floor

PLAN OF *VILLA RUSTICA* AT BOSCOREALE

wine was taken to a large open shed where it was left to ferment in great vats open to the sun and air, according to the custom of that part of Italy. In other smaller rooms there were presses for crushing olives and extracting the oil. Sleeping quarters for the slaves, a wagon-shed, and the threshing-floor completed the buildings of this particular farm. Its trade was evidently in wine and olives only, for in farms where cattle were bred there used to be a second courtyard, surrounded by stables.

IV

A TYPICAL DAY IN THE LIFE OF A ROMAN

PRACTICALLY all the work and recreation of a Roman had to be fitted into the hours of daylight, for the means of artificial lighting were most unsatisfactory. Small glimmering lamps illuminated the inside of buildings and the shop-fronts, but the streets were unlighted save by torches. It must be noted that the Roman hour (*hora*) was one-twelfth of the time from sunrise to sunset, and hence, though of varying length according to the time of the year—longer in summer than in winter—it was a definite space of time. Though the length of the day varied with the seasons, the number of hours (12) remained the same all the year round. (We are reminded by the parable of the labourers in the vineyard that the twelfth hour, i.e. sundown, marked

A ROMAN LAMP

the end of the day.) There were no mechanical clocks, but only sundials, hour-glasses, and water-clocks.

With such a lack of reliable means of dividing and marking the time, it is difficult to imagine how the Romans could be punctual. But life was simpler then than it is to-day, and they do not seem to have felt any inconvenience. The wealthy had a round of duties and amusements to fill the intervals between meals; for, as the poet Martial said, their stomachs

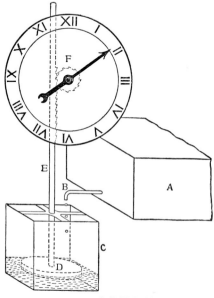

From the tank A water drips at a uniform rate through the small pipe B into the reservoir C in which is the float D. From the upper surface of D rises the shaft E the teeth of which, by their movement as the shaft rises, rotate the cog-wheel F. To this cog-wheel is attached a hand the position of which, on the surface of the dial, indicates the hour

A ROMAN WATER-CLOCK

were their best clocks. The poorer citizens led a somewhat idle life; so time meant little to them. Slaves worked from before daylight till they were released from their tasks, and therefore had no need to reckon the passing of time.

We must notice first of all that the Romans rose earlier than we do. Shops were opened at sunrise; boys were on their way to school in winter while it was still dark; and often a busy man had to deal with his correspondence and other personal affairs before daybreak, when a round of public duties would begin.

The first meal of the day would be eaten some time during the first two hours, while callers were gathering and the business of the day was beginning. This first meal was a light breakfast of the modern continental type—bread dipped in wine, or eaten with honey, olives, or cheese.

His meal finished, our well-to-do Roman would set out for the Forum, the centre of the city's commercial and business life. He would leave the house accompanied by the friends and clients who had come to pay him their respects, and no doubt would be joined by others on the way.

Clients were usually poor citizens or foreigners who had sought the protection of a more powerful citizen.

At the Forum a prominent citizen would find various duties sufficient to occupy the whole morning. There might be business in the law-courts; a sitting of the Senate to attend; a speech from the Rostra to deliver or to hear. If there was none of these, there were the crowds of citizens amongst whom lively discussions on politics or business were always to be found. Then at noon came lunch, which was a rather slighter meal than its modern equivalent.

As the Romans became more luxurious in their habits, their baths became more elaborate. At one period a swim in the Tiber had to content them; but in the course of time more and more splendid baths were built, especially by the Emperors. Seneca, writing to his friend Lucilius in the middle of the first century A.D., compares the simplicity of the 'good old days' of Cato with the luxury and self-indulgence of his own times. He mentions 'walls covered with huge, expensive mirrors, marble pilasters from Alexandria, set off by plaques of Numidian marble in between, with elaborate borders of picturesque design and variety of subject, a ceiling full of glass, silver taps and fittings, the margin of the bath made of Thasian marble'. Without all these the Romans of Seneca's day considered themselves poorly provided, though the bathing establishments made only a very small charge for admission and sometimes no charge at all.

The Stabian baths at Pompeii may be taken as typical of the baths of the later days of the Republic. In the middle there was an open court where gymnastic exercises might be taken before or after bathing. Adjoining this, on one side, there was a swimming bath. On the opposite side, in addition to waiting-rooms, there was first the undressing-room, furnished with benches, lockers, and niches, and then the *frigidarium* which contained a cold-water bath (sometimes large enough for swimming) surrounded by a tiled paving. Next there was the *tepidarium*, or warm-air room, followed by the *caldarium* which contained a hot-water bath. Originally the heat was supplied by braziers in the different rooms, but later there was a system of central heating by hot air from a single furnace.

The hot-air bath, which resembled the Turkish bath of to-day, was to be found also in the houses of the well-to-do; but in Imperial Rome every one from the Emperor downwards used the public baths.

The bath was taken about the ninth hour and it was followed by dinner, the chief meal of the day. This was more than just a meal; it was also the principal social function, to be enjoyed when the day's work was over and its duties were performed.

The meal itself consisted usually of only three courses. First came snacks of tasty food to whet the appetite; then the chief course, consisting of more solid fare, of which there would be several kinds, even as many as six or seven; and last of all, pastry and fruit. Sometimes the drinking of wine

'At the Forum a prominent citizen would find various duties sufficient to occupy the whole morning'
The 'Forum of Trajan' as it appeared in his day

was carried on after the end of the meal: this was another practice borrowed from the Greeks.

A ROMAN AT TABLE

Notice that he reclines on a couch with a small table by his side. He does not sit in a chair. His slave waits upon him

To the ordinary well-bred, educated Roman, however the eating of food was the least important part of the function; for though there were usually only the three courses, the meal lasted often for three English hours. The time was taken up with discussions upon current events, literature, philosophy, or politics. Cicero wrote in *De Senectute* that it had always been his way 'to measure the enjoyment of banquets as much by sociability and the delights of conversation as by their physical attractions'.

For greater comfort the guests reclined on couches (*triclinia*) at the table. The arrangement of the couches varied, but they were always placed so that conversation might be easily carried on. The accompanying sketch shows an ordinary way of placing the couches.

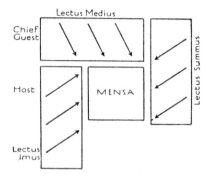

Walking shoes were removed on entering, sandals being worn in their place: 'to ask for one's shoes' came to be the regular expression for rising from the table. When the guests departed, their host would retire for the night.

In this outline of a typical day's occupations it will be noticed that there has been no mention of family life. The reason is that in the closing years of the Republic the family life which had been so valuable in building the character of the citizens was being undermined by public duties and outside interests. The family might meet at meal-times, especially at dinner if there were no guests; but otherwise the father of a family saw very little of his children.

The powers of the father (*paterfamilias*) were as great as those of the Old Testament patriarchs, like Abraham or Jacob. In the family circle these powers were equal to a king's, and included even the judgement of life and death.

There were reasons for this. The father was more than just the head of the family. Through him the life of the family was continued, and through him also were passed on the traditions and the personal qualities that make any family different from all others. He was the priest who attended to the family altars: he cast into the hearth-fire, sacred to Vesta, morsels of food left over from meals; he made sacrifices to the gods that guarded the household goods. It was his duty to teach his sons the religion of their forefathers; and at one time it had been the recognized thing for him to teach them the physical accomplishments (riding, swimming, wrestling, &c.) which were a part of every Roman's training. But as public life came to make more calls upon his time, the average citizen left the early training of his sons to his wife or, more usually, to slaves. This transfer of the father's duty cut at the very root of family life and went a long way to account for the decline of Roman character. Even when men like Cicero saw the danger they were powerless to prevent it; for Cicero complained that he had to leave the training of his son to other people, because, as he wrote once in a letter to his brother, at Rome 'he had no time to breathe'.

V

ROMAN DRESS

SINCE our knowledge of Roman dress is derived mainly from statues, reliefs on memorials, and remains of that kind, we shall find that pictures of monuments will make clear the main features of Roman clothes. At the outset we must remember that Italy enjoys a pleasanter and more sunny climate than our own, so that fewer garments were necessary to them than are necessary to us. In fact, we may say that amongst the Romans the increase in the number of articles of clothing was usually the mark of a dandy. In general, the

ROMAN DRESS
A cutler in a shop with a customer

Romans did not wear hats or stockings, though when the need arose similar garments (such as the hood of a cloak and puttees) were used.

The characteristic articles of men's clothing were two in number—the *tunica* and the *toga*. The first was a woollen garment like a rather long skirt, reaching below the knees as we can see in the picture of the cutler (p. 51). But it would be worn like this only when a man was taking his ease. Such a long garment would get in the way of a man at work; so it was ordinarily worn with a girdle or belt round the waist so that the *tunica* could be pulled up above the knees, as we see in the picture of the clothes-seller in his shop on p. 55. This picture shows that the *tunica* had short sleeves; in this respect it differed from the Greek pattern, which was usually sleeveless. Long sleeves reaching to the wrist were a mark of the dandy.

The *toga* was the distinctive garb of the Roman citizen. It was a dignified garment well in keeping with the Roman pride of race. It was not worn by workmen for the simple reason that it was so voluminous as to be a great hindrance to free movement and difficult to keep in order. Yet no Roman gentleman would think of appearing in public without his *toga*. In the picture of the tailor's shop (p. 55) we can see a customer wearing a *toga*. The same garment can be seen in greater detail in the picture of the bridegroom on p. 53. It was a strip of cloth about eighteen feet long and seven feet wide, with one curved edge and one straight edge, and was draped about the body in various ways.

Boys and men all wore the *toga*, as we can see in the picture of father and son on p. 57, but there were differences to mark the age or rank of the wearer. Boys up to the age of about sixteen years wore the *toga praetexta*, which had a purple stripe along the edge of it. This boyish garb was laid aside at the coming of manhood, when its place was taken by the plain white *toga virilis*. The *toga praetexta* was also worn by magistrates.

The *toga* was a fine dignified garment for ceremonies and for use in town, but it was unserviceable for campaigns. Then its place was taken by the military cloak called the *sagum.* This was so typical of the soldier's garb that 'to put on the *sagum*' was another way of saying 'to go to the wars'.

A ROMAN BRIDEGROOM AND HIS BRIDE

Various other cloaks were worn, especially by country people, travellers, and those who were out in all weathers. Such cloaks were usually of shaggy wool, and sometimes had a hood that could be drawn over the head in the event of rain. Usually a Roman went bare-headed. A conical hat known as a *pilleus* was sometimes worn. A white hat of this shape was the special mark of a freedman.

Turning to women's clothing we find that the Roman matron also wore a distinctive garb, the special features of which were the *stola* and the *palla*. The first took the place of the *tunica*, and was the traditional dress of a Roman lady. It reached the ground but could be raised by a girdle, worn rather high. It had sleeves reaching to the elbow. The *palla* was the feminine counterpart of the *toga*, and, like the *toga*, was the proper dress for outdoors. It was worn over the left shoulder, drawn across the back, then brought over or under the right shoulder and round the body. Sometimes the *palla*, which was generally rectangular in shape, was drawn over the head as protection from the weather: as mill-girls of to-day use headscarfs for the same purpose. When it was worn in the ordinary way the *palla* left the right arm free for movement.

VI

ROMAN BOYHOOD AND EDUCATION

On the ninth day after his birth, a Roman boy received his name with due ceremonies, in which both the family and the household slaves took part. Those present usually made gifts to the child of tiny models of everyday objects (swords, axes, &c.), which were strung together in the form of a necklace, and served as a kind of charm.

A more powerful protection against harm was the *bulla* that was hung round the baby boy's neck, and worn till he

An example of Roman hairdressing

Romans choosing material at a cloth factory, or perhaps a tailor's shop
A large sample is held up for their inspection by two slaves

reached manhood and put on the *toga virilis*. The *bulla*[1] was simply a metal locket containing a lucky charm or mascot, made of gold or bronze, according to the parents' means. It may be compared with the lock and chain of silver which are still put round the neck of a Chinese boy to lock in his life and keep him from harm.

A Roman boy received at least three names—the *praenomen*, *nomen*, and *cognomen*. The most important was the second, which showed to which *gens* or clan the boy belonged. This name always ended in *-ius*, as Julius, Fabius, Tullius.

The *praenomen* was the equivalent of our Christian name; and just as we often use only an initial for this, so with the older Roman names an initial was commonly used for the *praenomen*, as C. for Gaius, M. for Marcus, and so on. The less common names were always written in full.

The *cognomen* was a kind of family name, to show to which branch of a *gens* a person belonged. We usually know Romans by their *cognomen* (e. g. Caesar, Cicero, Scipio), though sometimes by the English form of the *nomen* (e.g. Horace, Ovid, Vergil). Often the third name showed originally some personal or physical trait, as did our surnames like Little, Short, and many others, and historical nicknames like Richard Crookback. An additional *cognomen* was sometimes conferred on a man to commemorate a great achievement. It was often given to soldiers. For instance, P. Cornelius Scipio Africanus received the last of his names on account of his successful wars in Africa. (We have seen the same thing happen in our own days. When titles were conferred on our generals and admirals at the end of the last war they were usually taken from the scenes of their most memorable actions

---

[1] In later times the box containing the Pope's seal was called a *bulla*, and the word was transferred to the document, the Papal Bull, to which the seal was attached.

FOUR STAGES IN THE UPBRINGING OF A ROMAN BOY

1. A baby in his mother's lap. 2. Carried by his father. 3. Aged six or seven, he drives in a small model of a chariot, drawn by a pet goat. 4. He is now at school, and is shown reciting something he has learned to his father

—e.g. Viscount Montgomery of Alamein, Earl Alexander of Tunis.) An additional *cognomen* was handed on to a man's eldest son, but he in turn could not pass it on.

As in all times and in all countries, a Roman boy spent his earliest years under his mother's care; but (in the first centuries of the Republic at any rate) the father took a share in his son's training as soon as the boy was beyond the stage of babyhood. Plutarch gives us the following delightful picture of the care that Cato bestowed on his son's upbringing. 'As soon as the dawn of intelligence began in his son, he decided to give his personal attention to his education. For, he tells us, if his son's progress happened to be slow, he had no intention of having him reprimanded, or pulled by the ear, by a servant; nor did he wish him to be indebted to a mean person for his education. So he taught him literature and law himself; and also the necessary sports, javelin-throwing, fighting hand to hand, riding, boxing, and swimming, even in rapid rivers, and the endurance of heat and cold. He also tells us that he wrote out stories for him, in large hand, to acquaint him with the romance and the traditions of his country.' In the early days, when the Romans were an agricultural people, the father would also instruct his son in the work of the farm.

At the age of seven, definite schooling began, though it is difficult to say exactly when schools were first set up in Rome. It is certain that for centuries the government thought that education was a private matter for parents to arrange. The first schoolmasters in Rome were usually Greeks. They were often freedmen who had received a certain amount of education, for slaves were by no means always illiterate (see Chap. XV). Aesop, the writer of fables, is a well-known example of an educated slave; and another is Tiro, Cicero's secretary. It is certain that the average Roman boy looked down on his teachers as being of lower class than himself. The schoolmasters enforced their authority by savage punishments. Boys were flogged for the smallest offences. Even in those days, impositions were often set. There were no special school buildings: a teacher received his pupils in a room open to the street that might have served as a shop, or sometimes in an upper room.

School began very early in the day. In winter boys were on their way thither before it was light, and the Roman poet, Juvenal, speaks of the books being blackened with smoke from the pupils' lanterns. The schoolboy ate his 'breakfast' on his way to school—usually a bun or a piece of bread, just as French schoolboys of to-day can be seen munching a roll for their breakfast as they go to school. There was an interval at midday, when the boy would go home to lunch.

To, from, and in school, and in fact at all times and in all places, a Roman boy of the better class was accompanied by a tutor (*paedagogus*), who was usually a Greek slave. The tutor was responsible to a great extent for the boy's manners and conduct, and, in addition, he gave the boy the chance of regular practice in speaking Greek. This practice was very useful, for, after the spread of Roman rule outside Italy, a man needed to know Greek as well as Latin, just as any one to-day with more than an elementary education has learned French or some other modern language.

Up to the middle of the third century B.C., practically the only subjects taught in the schools were reading, writing, and arithmetic. All calculations were done on the fingers (*digiti*)—whence our word 'digit' for numbers up to ten —or with an instrument called an *abacus*. The need for such an instrument for calculation arose from the awkward form of the Roman numerals. The illustration shows an *abacus*, though schoolboys would no doubt use a

simpler type, more like the bead-frames still used in China
for ordinary counting. We can disregard the five rods at the
right-hand side. They were used only for working fractions
of the duodecimal type—i.e. having the denominator a mul-
tiple of twelve. The other fourteen rods on the *abacus* were
for dealing with whole numbers. Thus, the rod marked I was
for counting units, the next (marked x) for tens, the next for
hundreds and so on up to millions, which were counted on

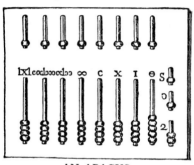

AN ABACUS

the extreme left-hand rod. It will be noticed that the seven
longer rods to the left had only four beads, so that it was
possible to count on them only as far as 4, 40, 400 . . . as the
case might be. The one bead on each short rod stood for five
units, tens, hundreds, and so on; and thus the process of
counting was made more rapid. Even so, it was a difficult
instrument to use, especially for division and multiplication.
The earliest *abaci* simply had grooves in which pebbles
(*calculi*) could be moved along; from this we derive our
modern word 'calculate'.

Writing exercises consisted of copying numerous proverbs
and moral maxims, of which more than seven hundred are
still known. They were also learned by heart for repetition.
Spelling was fairly easy, because Latin was pronounced as

it was spelt. This elementary education went on till a boy was about twelve years of age, when he went on to a school of a higher kind.

The more advanced schools had come into being as part of the imitation of Greek ways which changed so many of Roman ideas, from about 250 B.C. onwards. Not only was the Greek language introduced into them, but also the study of Greek literature, especially the works of Homer. The teachers in these were Greeks. They were called *grammatici*, and from them we derive the term 'grammar' as used of schools to-day.

In addition to Greek language and literature, Latin literature was also studied. The poems of Horace were used as school-texts even in his own lifetime, in the same way as the works of contemporary writers are used in our own schools to-day. The most important subject taught in the schools was rhetoric, i.e. the art of public speaking. When all free citizens had a direct share in the government and a vote, rhetoric was a very important branch of study. To be able to speak cleverly and well, to stir up people's feelings, in the law-courts or on the Rostra, was a great help to public success. Every schoolboy knows how the Roman mob was swayed by the artful oratory of Mark Antony over the dead body of Caesar. The study of public speaking was often carried on after the rest of the boy's school-days were over. For this subject, there was a special master called a *rhetor*.

Roman schoolboys had numerous holidays. Every ninth day (the *nundinae* or market day) was a recognized holiday, as well as certain of the great religious festivals, more especially the Saturnalia in December, a time of great festivities like our Christmas holidays, and the festival of Minerva in the third week of March. In country schools, the summer months were kept as holidays, for the boys were required to work during the gathering of the olives and the grapes. We find something similar in modern London when East End schools are closed for a week or two in the autumn while the children are away for the hop-picking; and similar 'blackberry weeks' are well known in the North. In Rome itself, the climate was so unhealthy in August and September that schools were usually closed while the pupils went away with the parents, in much the same way as the children of European residents in India went with their parents to the hill-stations at certain seasons. As the poet Martial said, it was enough in those months for a boy to learn to keep well.

The school materials were quite different from those that we use. Paper was expensive; so most written exercises were worked on wax tablets, that could be smoothed and used again and again, like the slates formerly used in some English schools. Instead of a pen, a sharp instrument (*stilus*) was used for making the letters. Later on, a boy might be allowed to use paper (made from the Egyptian papyrus plant) and ink; but even so it would be what we should call waste paper, since it had already been used on one side for some other purpose before being brought to school.

Books were in the form of rolls. At first they were made from the pith of the papyrus reed, and from the name of this (*liber*) came the Latin word for a book. Later on parchment was used. The writing—there were, of course, no printed books—was arranged in columns from the top to the bottom of the breadth of the roll. The reader held his 'book' in both hands, rolling up with his left and unrolling with his right as he read. From this action of unrolling we have our word 'volume' as applied to a book (Latin verb *volvere*). For reading, two or three columns of writing would be unrolled at one time. The rolls (if there were many of them, as in a library) were stored in pigeon-holes or in circular open boxes.

Books were copied entirely by hand, and every educated Roman kept a number of slaves whose sole duty was the copying of books. Of course, mistakes in copying were often made. Once a book had been written, any one who could get

ANCIENT WRITING MATERIALS

hold of it might make as many copies as he wished, and in this way writers had very small returns for their work.

Till the time of Augustus there were no public libraries in Rome, though just before his death Julius Caesar had made arrangements for the founding of one. Wealthy men who had private libraries often allowed scholars to use their books for purposes of study. The famous orator, Cicero, for example, had the use of the magnificent library of his wealthy patron Lucullus.

The education of a Roman boy was no more finished within the walls of the schoolroom than is the education of a boy to-day. A Roman had much to learn of politics and social affairs; so, while still a lad, he often accompanied his father to gain an idea of the work and duties that would be his in later years. He would go with his father to the Forum, the law-courts, and the Senate-house, to the temples to learn

A relief of about A.D. 150, showing a schoolmaster seated between two pupils (who hold Roman 'books' or rolls). The third boy is late, and is being scolded by his master

the religious rites, and to dinner-parties to hear the talk of men of affairs. In this way he would be well equipped to take his place as a citizen, when the time came for him to put away boyish things and take upon himself the ways of manhood.

His coming-of-age was marked by special ceremonies. It took place somewhere between the end of the fourteenth and the beginning of the seventeenth years of age. The exact time seems to have been fixed by the father, but it must at latest have been before the youth was liable to serve in the army, i.e. when he was seventeen years old. The ceremony took the form of a family festival. The parents and friends of the boy accompanied him to the Forum and thence to the Capitoline Hill, where sacrifice was offered in the Temple of Jupiter. The *bulla* was left there with other boyish things, and instead of the purple-edged toga the youth now put on the *toga virilis* (from *vir*, a man) of manhood. No doubt St. Paul, himself a Roman, had this ceremony in mind when he wrote the well-known words—'when I became a man, I put away childish things'.

VII

PUBLIC AMUSEMENTS

In the earliest days the great shows given in the Roman circus were connected with religious worship. As time passed the connexion became slighter; and by the end of the Republic it became the regular custom to commemorate this or that event or person by public games. Days were definitely set aside for the games in the calendar. Under the Empire nearly half the year was taken up with these official holidays, so that in the end their number had to be limited. Not only were great public games organized by the rulers of the city, but also they were given by private individuals, often to increase their popularity amongst the citizens. These private shows were usually quite as elaborate and costly as the official entertainments.

The oldest games in the calendar were known as the *ludi magni* or *ludi Romani*. They seem first to have been held during the days of the kings, and they were commonly observed in early times to celebrate a victory of the Roman armies. As time went on, however, these games came to be held regularly every autumn, even if there were no victory to celebrate. Sulla was the first general who celebrated his victories with public games, and his example was followed by Julius Caesar, Augustus, and many of the Emperors. The military origin survived in the custom of opening these games with a procession copied from that of a triumph, described in another chapter.

The *ludi magni* were connected with the worship of Jupiter. Other games called *ludi plebeii* were also held in his honour, and there were still others in honour of rustic deities like Flora and Ceres.

The public shows and games were very varied in character, but they may be classified in three groups—the *Ludi Circenses*, which included chariot races and all contests that took place in a circus; the *Ludi Scaenici*, or dramatic entertainments; and the *Munera Gladiatoria*, or prize-fights.

By far the most popular were the games in the circus. The *Circus Maximus* was an immense rectangle with semi-circular ends, surrounded with covered seats on tiers, and furnished with special 'boxes' for the officials and magistrates. The open space in the middle was called the arena from the sand that covered it. Lengthwise along the arena, and not exactly in the middle, was a dividing barrier known as the *spina*, often consisting of a row of statues on a long marble base. At each end of the *spina* were set three conical pillars that marked the turning-points in the races. Here also were placed seven egg-shaped objects made of marble, or seven dolphins— the former being the symbols of the twins Castor and Pollux, and the latter of Neptune, all of whom were patron deities of horse-racing. One of these marble eggs or dolphins was removed each time a lap in a race was finished, for the guidance of the charioteers.

Chariot races were the most popular entertainments in the *Circus Maximus*, and those who have seen the film version

The Colosseum at Rome, in which gladiatorial shows, sham fights, great hunts of wild animals, and every sort of spectacle took place. It was possible to seat about 50,000 spectators in this enormous amphitheatre

Roman relief showing a fight in the arena between gladiators and wild beasts. At the ...

of *Ben Hur* can well realize how exciting these races became. There were usually seven laps in a single race, and there might be as many as twenty-four races in one day. Just as to-day in horse-racing the jockeys wear the special colours of the owners, so the charioteers in the Roman circus wore the colours of the companies for whom they worked and who contracted for the supply of charioteers. There were four companies, distinguished by the colours white, red, blue, and green. It is curious to note that these colours came to have a political meaning, and the word for the contracting companies (*factiones*) gives us our word 'faction', which means a political party.

The charioteers had to be extremely skilful, especially in turning at the ends of the *spina*, where there was always the danger of a collision when the chariots bunched together. The costume of a charioteer can be seen on page 71. It will be noticed that the ends of the reins were wound round the man's body, and he carried a sharp knife with which to cut the reins if the chariot overturned, an accident that might easily happen since the chariot was built very light. Successful charioteers earned very large sums of money, and there are records of men making fortunes that can be counted in millions of sesterces.

Before a race began the chariots and horses waited in small vaulted chambers known as *carceres*. These were provided with folding doors that were flung wide open by attendant slaves when the starting-signal was given by the presiding magistrate, who waved a white cloth for the purpose. The winning-post was marked by a broad white line in front of the magistrate's *tribunal*.

The day's racing was always preceded by a procession, from the Capitol to the Circus Maximus. At the head of the procession came the magistrate in charge of the games.

He rode in a chariot if he were a consul or a praetor, and was dressed in the style of a triumphing general. After him came his supporters, and troops of noble youths on foot and horseback. They were followed first by a host of competitors, and then by priests with incense, sacred vessels, and images of the gods. This procession made its way all round the circus and finished at the magistrate's box.

There were other shows in the circus beside horse-racing. Such were the baiting of wild beasts, and mimic hunts, when trees were planted in the arena to resemble a forest. Magistrates were always on the look-out for new thrills to please the spectators, and money was lavishly spent for that purpose. Julius Caesar brought large numbers of unfamiliar wild beasts to Rome to fight in the circus. Another form of entertainment was a mimic sea-fight, the arena being first flooded so that the ships could float.

There is less to be said about the dramatic performances, since these were largely borrowed from the Greeks and never became very popular in Rome. A play with a regular plot and a definite dialogue was called a *fabula*; more popular, however, were the farces and dumb-shows. In the farces much of the dialogue was made up on the spur of the moment, like the 'patter' of modern music-hall comedians, and depended for its success upon topical references and a spice of vulgarity to please the lower orders. The dumb-shows (*pantomimi*) were remarkable because there was no spoken dialogue in them, but the whole story or plot was unfolded by means of actions alone.

The gladiatorial shows are rightly considered as a blot on Roman civilization. In early times they were private affairs, but they came to be a popular form of public spectacle. While foreign wars were being waged there were always slaves in abundance who could be 'butchered to make a Roman holiday'. The gladiators were nearly always foreigners, for very few Romans took up this kind of fighting as a profession.

The men were herded in great barracks while they were

A CHARIOT RACE IN THE CIRCUS

The driver on the left has just come to the turning-point, marked by the *metae*

being trained to fight against each other or against wild beasts. There were various kinds of fights between gladiators, but one of the most popular was that between the *retiarius* and the *secutor*. The former wore no armour, but carried a net (*rete*) and a dagger; the latter was fully armed. The *retiarius* or net-carrier tried to entangle his opponent in the net and so to throw him. If he failed he would have to run from the attack of his armed opponent, whose name *secutor* means literally the 'follower'. In any of these combats when one man was at the mercy of the other, his life depended on the favour of the crowd. The victor appealed to the audience. If the defeated gladiator was popular or had put up a good fight, he might be spared; if not, the fatal sign was

TWO GLADIATORS PRACTISING
Their trainer stands behind them, giving them instruction

made by thrusting down the thumb, and the wretched victim was promptly slain. In theory the sign was given by the presiding magistrate, but he always acted in deference to the wishes of the crowd. These hideous butcheries finally came to an end when Christianity stirred the better feelings of the Romans.

VIII

MARRIAGE AND FUNERAL CUSTOMS

LIKE all nations the Romans had their special customs in connexion with the chief events of family life—birth, marriage, and death. In an earlier chapter we have traced the customs connected with childhood and youth up to the time when a man came of age and put on the *toga virilis*.

By that time he was probably engaged to be married, since betrothals might be arranged at any age above the seventh year. The Romans were a hard, unsentimental people, and their marriages were often merely legal contracts between families. Even so there were superstitions and customs connected with the actual ceremony. For example, it was thought unlucky to be married during the month of May, while June was regarded as a lucky month. It is interesting to remember that both these superstitions still survive to-day.

The details of the marriage ceremonies varied, but as time went on there was a tendency to make them more and more simple. Only for priests or those who held high office was the most elaborate ceremony used. This was called *confarreatio*, from the fact that the bride and bridegroom ate together a cake made from the grain called spelt (*far*), and it was accompanied by solemn sacrifices and the taking of auspices. The usual ceremony was that of *coemptio*, which consisted chiefly of the exchange of coins as a sign of the contract.

The customs connected with the wedding-day mainly concerned the bride. She wore a special dress and a marriage veil of yellow hue, since that colour was sacred to Hymen, the god of marriage. Her hair was parted with a spear's point before being plaited—a reminder, perhaps, of the old days when the Romans carried off the Sabine women by force of

arms to be their wives. At evening, a procession set forth to
the bridegroom's house, the way being lighted by youths
carrying torches. Having reached her new home, the bride
was carried over the threshold by her husband, perhaps to
prevent the chance of an ill-omened stumble. Next she was
given the keys of the store-cupboards, and two vessels containing fire and water, to signify that she was now in charge
of all household duties. Then followed the marriage-feast,
and the ceremonies were over, except that on the next day
the young wife offered sacrifice for the first time at the family
shrine in her new home.

The Roman housewife (*matrona*) held an important position
in the home. She was regarded as the wife and mother of
Roman citizens, and as such she was held in greater honour
than the women of any other people in ancient times, except
perhaps the Spartans. She ranked as the equal of her husband, as we can see by the curious phrase used in the
marriage ceremony: *ubi ego Gaius, tu Gaia* (where I am
master, you are mistress).

In the early days of the Empire things had changed, no
doubt, but Romans were able to look back to the 'good old
times' when mothers had done so much in training their
sons in the virtues most valued by the Romans. Cornelia, the
mother of the Gracchi, was a noble example of the Roman
matron. She trained her sons to think of the welfare of the
State, so that when the elder one, Tiberius, became a man he
set himself to try to put right things that were hurtful to
the people as a whole. This made him unpopular and he
lost his life. Cornelia, however, did nothing to turn his
younger brother, Gaius, from following the same well-
meaning but fatal line of action when he was old enough to
continue his brother's work. Shakespeare has made for ever
famous the mother of Coriolanus, the ideal Roman matron.

It was her training and her delight in his valour that made Coriolanus excel. 'The only thing that made him to love honour was the joy he saw his mother did take of him,' as we read in Plutarch. In everything Volumnia guided the thoughts and acts of Coriolanus. It was her noble influence over him that led him to make peace with his own people after he had invaded Roman territory with a Volscian army. To withdraw meant a great blow to his pride, but he did so because of his mother's patriotic influence. It was the splendid character of matrons of the earlier days that largely helped to the building up of what was best and strongest in the Roman people.

The Romans were always very careful to see that their dead received fitting burial: for they believed that otherwise the spirits (*manes*) of the dead could not gain admittance to the underworld and so would return to haunt them. So strongly did they hold this belief that if by chance a man saw the body of a stranger who had met a violent or accidental death, he would cast upon the corpse three handfuls of earth as a symbolical act lest the spirits should trouble him. And if a man were drowned at sea, the same honours would be paid to an empty tomb as at the tomb of one who had been buried with all due ceremony.

Ordinary folk were, of course, not able to arrange for the elaborate rites that went with the burial of a rich or prominent man, but nothing was omitted that could be reasonably done. People of moderate means often subscribed amongst themselves to buy a burial-place that could be used in common, to make sure of a suitable resting-place for their ashes.

When the body was prepared for burial, it was clothed in the same style as during life. Those who had borne any public office in the State or gained any honour in war were, after their death, wrapped in the particular garment belonging to their rank and adorned with the crowns or other honours they had won. The corpse was then laid on a funeral couch in the *atrium*, with the feet towards the door—so that the spirits should know only the way out. A bough of cypress or pine was set up outside the door as a sign of mourning.

Seven days after death usually elapsed before the actual burial. During that time the ceremony of *conclamatio* took place—i.e. crying aloud the name of the dead, either to recall the soul or to reawaken its powers. When there was no response, the dead was said to be *conclamatus*, beyond recall. In early times funerals took place by night (whence undertakers were called *vespillones*, from *vesper*, the evening), but later on the morning was commonly the appointed time, especially for public funerals. As a reminder of the custom of burial by night, lighted torches were carried even by daytime in the funeral procession.

The size and composition of this procession varied, of course, according to the rank of the dead; but with all classes of people every effort was made to have the procession as imposing as possible. Apart from the mourners, there were musicians with pipes and trumpets, and men who mimicked the actions of the dead man, and even his voice and personal peculiarities. The waxen effigies of ancestors were carried out, and, at a public funeral, tableaux to represent events in the dead man's life. If he had held public office the lictors were there, carrying their rods reversed, as soldiers reverse their rifles at a military funeral to-day. There were also hired mourners, women who made loud lamentations, tearing their hair and beating their breasts, like the Jewish women whom Jesus found in the house of Jairus, weeping and wailing, as the Gospels relate. Finally came all and sundry who joined

A ROMAN FUNERAL

The body of the deceased is fully dressed and is carried on a litter borne by eight men. In front goes a band of flute (below), trumpet, and horn players. A crowd of hired mourners and relatives accompanies the body the procession from motives of respect or curiosity: at the public funeral of a great man, vast numbers would be found in this last part of the procession. It may be noted that the same practice exists in France at the present time. Notices of a death are posted up publicly, with a general request to all friends, acquaintances, and sympathizers to join in the funeral procession, which is always on foot, as in ancient Rome; and in North Country villages of England the 'bidders' (usually relatives of the deceased) go round inviting people to the funeral. At a public funeral, the procession made its way to the Forum, where a speech was delivered from the Rostra by a relation or friend of the deceased. When Mark Antony is made to say

'I come to bury Caesar, not to praise him,'

the second half of the statement is no more than an orator's trick, for a speech of praise was expected upon all such occasions. (This is another Roman funeral custom that is still observed in France.) Such speeches were sometimes made in honour of women; for, as Plutarch tells us, the Senate granted them this privilege when the women of Rome gave their golden ornaments to be melted down for the gift that was sent to the temple of Delphi after the capture of Veii.

The burial-places, except those of the Vestal Virgins, were always outside the city, as in Greece and amongst the Jews; and they were usually near the public highways. Travellers to Rome can still see the ruins of great tombs along both sides of the Appian Way.

It was the custom to burn the body, and the funeral pyre, in the shape of an altar, was usually set very near the tomb. The bier on which the body lay was placed on top of the pyre, and then the nearest relation set a lighted torch to the dry resinous wood. As a mark of respect and affection, costly offerings of garments, perfumes, and sweet-smelling essences were thrown into the flames. When the pyre had burned down, the ashes were cooled with wine and gathered into an urn which was then placed in the tomb. There were several kinds of tombs; a common type that still survives in our

A COLUMBARIUM
On the Appian Way, near Rome

churchyards is like an altar. Many tombstones have been preserved and are to be seen in most of the larger museums. Often the effigy of the dead person was carved in relief upon the stone. There is, for example, a well-known tombstone from the grave of a surgeon. He is shown reading, and above the case containing his rolls there is a case of surgical instruments indicating his profession. Sometimes the tomb was a family sepulchre, a simple building of brick or stone, in which the mortal remains of all the members of one family would be placed in urns in niches round the walls. To the present day the same practice is observed in the island of Corsica, where there are no cemeteries, but instead mortuary chapels along the roadsides just outside every town and village. Not every Roman family had money enough to build its own sepulchre, however, and so it was a common practice for several families to combine to build a sepulchre that could be used by all of them. All round the walls inside were niches to hold the urns, with a small slab giving the dead person's name under each. From its likeness to a dove-cot, such a tomb was called a *columbarium* (from *columba*, a dove).

The memory of the dead was kept alive by certain festivals, especially the Parentalia in February. There were as well commemorative feasts. Offerings were made in the form of libations of water, wine, milk, blood, and sweet-smelling balms, poured out on or near the tomb; while flowers were scattered, and garlands were twined round the urn. The feasts were both public and private. The first were simply great banquets, accompanied often by a distribution of free food to the poorer people. They were held in honour only of the great. But all except the poorest arranged private feasts for relatives and friends, on the lines of the wakes that are still held in Ireland and Lancashire. A feast was prepared for the dead as well. On the tomb were placed dishes of beans, bread, and eggs, for the spirits to come and eat; and what was not consumed was burnt at the tomb.

IX

TRADE AND MONEY

WE have already seen that at first the Romans were settlers on the land, drawing their living from the soil and counting their wealth in flocks and herds. In the early days, every family could live practically on what it produced, and anything beyond bare necessities was obtained by barter. But gradually this state of things was changed, owing to the development of town life and the raising of the general standard of living with the growing wealth of Rome.

The people who drifted into the towns naturally could not produce food and other necessities of life for themselves. There developed, in consequence, a system of trading in the ordinary produce of the land between the towns and the country. More and more, too, the Romans were forced to trade with other nations. Their trade was not, like ours, concerned with manufactured goods, since every town had its own craftsmen working at their separate trades.

The destruction of Corinth and of Carthage in a single year (147–146 B.C.) removed the two greatest trade rivals that Rome had had and opened to her the markets of the whole Mediterranean. She was not slow to take advantage of her opportunity. In a very little while Rome had complete control of the profitable slave-trade that was centred in the Aegean island of Delos; and the produce of all the Mediterranean lands was gathered up to satisfy the increasing demands of Roman luxury. Nor was the enterprise of the Romans limited to the countries bordering the inland sea. It is interesting to find that the Romans made use of overland trading routes to the Far East, some of which remained in Italian control throughout the Middle Ages. We hear of silks being brought from China by way of Turkestan and the River Euphrates, and spices from Ceylon and the Malabar coast.

The two chief ports for Rome were Puteoli, on the Bay of Naples, and Ostia, at the mouth of the Tiber. In Rome the earliest trading centre was along the quays near the old cattle market, the Forum Boarium. Here in very early days there was an important trade in salt, of which we are reminded by the name of the *Via Salaria* which ran from Rome to the salt-marshes near Ostia. After the reduction of Carthage and the cities of Greece, the trade of Rome became so considerable that the quays and warehouses along the river-bank were greatly enlarged to deal with the merchandise coming up the river from Ostia. The shops were cleared out of the Forum Boarium to give room for business on the lines of a modern Stock Exchange. The commercial district was known as the Emporium,[1] and all kinds of goods were brought to Rome to be stored in its warehouses. Grain from Egypt, oil and wine from Greece and Gaul, salt from Picenum, metals from Spain, and marble from Greece and Africa were the most important. It is interesting to remember that in these days we give the name *Emporium* to those huge stores where every kind of articles may be bought.

There were also markets where the ordinary shopkeepers could buy their stock-in-trade. Thus the Forum Holitorium was the market for the greengrocers. In other parts of the city there was a tendency for traders in particular wares to congregate in certain streets, as they do in modern London.

With all this varied and considerable trade there came, naturally enough, a system of coinage. There were no coins in the earliest days. People obtained what they needed by barter, and it is said that for such purposes twelve sheep were reckoned the equivalent of a cow. Certain it is that cattle were taken as the basis of exchange, and from the Latin word *pecus* (cattle) was derived the word *pecunia* for money.

The earliest form of money as such was simply a bar of copper of a standard weight, namely a pound (*libra*). From

[1] It should be noted that this name, like most of the Roman words connected with trade, was of Greek origin.

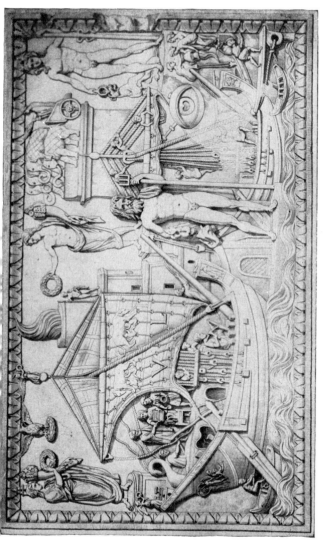

AN ITALIAN HARBOUR

A scene on a bas-relief. A large merchant ship is arriving on the left, and on the right a smaller one is unloading a cargo of wine-jars. Between them is a statue of Neptune. The sculptor probably meant to represent the harbour of Ostia

this is derived the modern French word for a pound (*la livre*).
Our sign £ (=L) represents the first letter of the same word.
The old idea of barter was still kept in mind by stamping
the bar with the impression of a cow.

It was not until the early third century B.C. that the
Romans first introduced a real coinage. For trading with
Greeks and other foreigners they struck silver coins called
didrachms, but for ordinary commerce they continued to
use coins made of bronze. This was now cast in the form of
a coin called an *as*, and in five smaller coins representing
fractions of an *as* ranging from one-half to one-twelfth.
(The smallest of these was called an *uncia*, whence we get
our words 'ounce' and 'inch', also a twelfth part). These
six bronze coins each bore on the obverse the head of a god,
and on the reverse there was a design of a ship's prow: so
that, instead of calling 'heads or tails' when he tossed a coin,
a Roman boy called *capita aut navim* (heads or ship).

The value of the *as* varied from time to time. Originally,
as a lump of metal, it weighed a pound of twelve ounces,
and so it remained until about 220 B.C. But during the war
with Hannibal, when things were going very badly for the
Romans, the *as* was reduced in weight. Probably in 214 B.C.,
they abandoned the old silver coins, and introduced a new kind
called the *denarius*; by again reducing the *as* to two ounces,
they were able to make the *denarius* equal to ten bronze *asses*.

From this time on, the silver and bronze coins were used
alongside one another, as in our own coinage, and they had
fixed values. The main coin was the silver *denarius* and its
less common fractions, the *quinarius* (of five *asses*) and the
sestertius (of 2½ *asses*). But the *as* fell slowly to about an
ounce in weight, until in 90 B.C. it was finally fixed at
one half-ounce; and the *denarius* was retariffed, i.e. it was
decreed that it should have a new value of sixteen *asses* and

the *sestertius* of four *asses*. This system remained in use for a long time. The *denarius* was the Roman 'penny' in the Bible, but we must remember that it was a silver coin. There were very few gold coins until the time of Julius Caesar.

It is rather difficult to assign an exact value to these coins. The most that can be done is to take good specimens of the actual coins and, by weighing them and testing the quality

Heads or Ship?

A Roman bronze *as*, enlarged (true size about 1¼ in. diam.). On the left is the obverse of the coin, showing Janus's head (for Janus see chap. xvii), and on the right the reverse, the prow of a ship

of their metal, to reckon an equivalent value in modern money. In this way a *denarius* of the first century B.C. can be reckoned as worth eightpence in modern money. From this estimate the values of the rest can be calculated. It should be noted that sums of money were usually counted by *sestertii*, and so a rough and ready way of turning such amounts into modern values is simply to count the *sestertius* as being worth twopence, so that 120 *sestertii* would be approximately the same as a pound in our money.

Though it is possible to give the rough equivalent values of these coins as coins, it must be remembered that we know but little about the purchasing value of Roman money, and what we do know about money in one part of the Empire would not necessarily apply to all parts.

X

SLAVERY

THOUGH slavery existed in Rome from the earliest times it was not till after the great wars of the third and second centuries B.C. that it became so widespread as to be a serious problem to the State. In the early days, when the Romans were a race of farmers, the members of the household (*familia*) who worked together to till the land comprised both bond and free. The bondmen had a definite position, and their lot (like that of the villeins in medieval England) was not unduly harsh.

This state of affairs was greatly changed by the successful wars of Rome. The army became a profession, and the increase of wealth and luxury led to the decay of the old-time virtues of simple living and hard work. There is a favourite story told of Cincinnatus that shows how the Romans admired the good old ways. It is said that when a Roman army was in great peril during a war with the Aequi in 458 B.C., the Senate sent for Cincinnatus to act as dictator and save the country. The messengers found the old man ploughing his fields with a team of oxen. He left the plough at the bidding of the Senate, and became dictator. In the short space of sixteen days he rescued the army from its dangerous position and, his task being accomplished, he laid down the dictatorship. He did not think it beneath his dignity to go back to work on his farm, whence he was called yet again twenty years later to be dictator a second time.

In those early days manual labour was not beneath the dignity of a Roman citizen, but in later times such work was thought undignified for the citizens of a great power like Rome. This change in outlook was brought about by the ever-increasing number of prisoners of war that provided cheap slave-labour, especially on the large country estates. The slaves were nearly always foreigners (*barbari*, non-Romans), but occasionally a Roman citizen might be condemned to be sold into slavery as the punishment for serious offences.

It is necessary to distinguish between the different types of slaves. The household slaves, especially those in the towns, were often Greeks of very good type and sometimes well educated—better educated, in fact, than their masters. They carried out many different duties, commercial and domestic; they acted as secretaries and copyists of books, and were put in charge of the sons of the family. Men carrying out such work must have been of some position and considerable education, and we may assume that, apart from their not being free, their position was little different from that of the humbler working-class citizens.

The slaves employed on the great country estates were very different from those in the town households. They were often Gauls or Spaniards by birth, wild and dangerous men, unwilling workers, who toiled in gangs like convicts, sometimes chained together, and usually locked in dungeon-like barracks by night. Those that worked on the sheep-farms of Southern Italy lived a wild life, and the fact that they were often armed for the defence of their flocks made them all the more dangerous. These slaves were in a constant state of discontent and always ready to rise in revolt. In this way they were a standing source of danger to the State, and this danger became very real on certain occasions. Thus at the revolt of Spartacus in 72–71 B.C., for months the consular armies were defied even to the point of defeat by rebellious slaves.

The Romans thought of a slave as being in the absolute power of his owner, who might even put him to death. He was not so much a person as a thing. An injury done to a slave was regarded as a wrong done to his master; yet, on the principle that more work could be got from a willing than from an unwilling slave, owners were not in the habit of taking advantage of their powers. Still, though slaves received reasonable treatment, they were the absolute property of their master. If a slave had no name of his own, his master's name would often be given to him, with the ending *-por*, standing for *puer* (boy); e. g. the slave of Marcus would be called Marcipor. (We are reminded that native household servants in Africa are still called 'boys' though they may be full-grown men.) Slaves dressed in much the same style as the poorer free citizens, except that they might wear a badge or might be branded as the punishment for some offence.

It has been calculated that there were about 200,000 slaves at the time of Cicero. This comparatively large number was due to the successful wars that had been waged during the last two centuries B.C. Slave-dealers actually accompanied the armies to buy and sell again the prisoners of war after every battle. On one occasion Julius Caesar had 53,000 captives sold after a victory. Slave-raiding also took place, Julius Caesar himself being carried off by pirates when a youth. The trade became so great that a regular market for slaves was established in the island of Delos, in the Aegean Sea. In Rome itself, the slaves were sold by auction, like cattle, as negroes were sold in America before slavery was abolished. As the number of slaves increased, no doubt they became cheaper to buy, and more and more slaves were used. Thus

Cato in the second century B.C. considered that only sixteen slaves were needed to work a vineyard of 100 acres; yet a century later Horace thought that every ordinary household

Manumission by the rod

A broken fragment of a bas-relief, showing a slave kneeling at the magistrate's feet, while the *lictor* (in the centre) touches him with a rod. On the left is another slave, who has just been freed, and is shaking hands with his master

needed at least ten slaves, and in most cases the number was very much larger.

Slaves might gain their freedom in various ways. Often a slave would buy his freedom out of his savings; often the master would free his slaves in gratitude for his services or other reasons. The ceremony of manumission or setting a slave free was as follows. The master went with his slave

to a magistrate and in his presence went through a curious
ceremony. The slave, wearing a special white cap called the
pilleus, knelt at the magistrate's feet, and a lictor touched him
with a rod, declaring him to be free. Thereupon the master
struck him with his hand, as a sign of the power he once had
over the slave but was now willingly giving up. It is curious
to note that the ceremony of dubbing a knight by striking
him with a sword probably has its origin in this ceremony
of 'manumission by the rod', as it was called.

There were less formal ways of setting a slave free. A
master might write a letter giving him his freedom, or invite
him to sit at table with him, or merely declare him free in the
presence of a few friends.

XI

ROADS AND TRAVEL

TRAVEL in the Roman world was an easier undertaking than
it was for centuries after the Roman Empire had fallen. This
was due not only to the strong government that maintained
the *pax Romana*, but also to the wonderful roads that were
made and kept up by that government. Roads were needed
by armies and officials and traders, and from the time that
Appius Claudius planned in 312 B.C. the road that bore his
name (the *Via Appia*), a network of great highways was made
to the farthest limits of the Empire.

Roads were built on a large scale from the time of Augustus
onwards, but even at the end of the Republic great main roads
led to all parts of Italy and another crossed Greece from the
west to Macedonia. It was the literal truth that 'all roads led
to Rome', and along them the legions marched, officials went
about the work of government, and traders brought merchan-

dise from the ends of the earth. It is scarcely too much to say that the Roman roads were the best lines of communication till railways came into being.

The first purpose of these roads was military. The Appian Way, for instance, was built to secure the Roman hold on Campania. As the rule of Rome spread farther, the great roads were established to make possible the work of government and defence. They were dead straight, for often the legions might need to move rapidly from one place to another. In consequence, the Romans gave little heed to natural obstacles. Their engineers were most skilful in overcoming difficulties—whether in bridging great rivers or in carrying the roadway across valleys by long viaducts. Throughout the Middle Ages the methods of Roman engineers were copied, and they are used by us to-day. The great public roads usually bore the name of the censor, consul, or emperor who caused them to be built. They were kept in repair by contractors at the expense of the government, though neighbouring landowners had to pay something towards their upkeep.

The early roads were probably earthen tracks, the surface of which was strengthened with stones. The roads typical of later times were called *viae munitae* (or *stratae*), and had a paved surface. There were usually five layers or courses in a *via munita*. The foundation was of earth rammed hard. On this were laid stones large enough to fill the hand. On top of them were smaller stones mixed with lime, covered with a layer of fine cement. The curved top layer was made of polygonal blocks of basalt or other suitable stone found in the neighbourhood. If the roads were built on a rocky foundation (e.g. parts of the Via Appia) only the two topmost layers were needed.

Milestones (*miliaria*) were a special feature of the Roman roads. These were first set up on a regular system by Caius

Gracchus, and afterwards they were erected all along the roads. They marked the distances from Rome, and sometimes from other important towns. In the Forum at Rome, Augustus set up the *Miliarium Aureum* from which the roads of Italy radiated. It was less a milestone than an indicator of distances from Rome to a number of important places.

The remains of Augustus's 'Golden milestone' (*miliarium aureum*) in the Forum at Rome

Bridges and viaducts were built where necessary, and in the south of France especially there still remain splendid specimens, almost intact after nearly 2,000 years. They were massive, like all Roman buildings, that were intended to impress by their very size. What is most remarkable about them is that they were usually made of blocks of stone so accurately cut that they held together without the use of cement, though sometimes the blocks would be clamped together with iron. The great Pont du Gard near Avignon supplies a striking reminder of the skill of Roman builders.

We can well imagine the numerous travellers that used these roads. Travel was in some respects easier and less restricted in those days than now, because the same Latin language was current all along the roads and a citizen would be under the same government though he travelled from Gaul to Greece. Many of the travellers were bent on government business—armies on the march; officials travelling in leisurely style with their retinues; embassies from subject tribes; messengers hastening with dispatches and official correspondence. Under the Empire there was a regular imperial post, with relays of horses, and post-houses for the letter-carriers. But this postal service was only for public business. All private letters were taken by couriers, employed privately. We can read in Cicero's letters how he took the opportunity of writing to friends when he heard of a trusty courier who was going their way. Learned men were amongst the crowds on the great roads, for there was more of a real commonwealth of learning when all men spoke the same tongue than in these days when there is the barrier of different languages. Well-to-do youths, like Caesar and Cicero, might be found making the 'Grand Tour' of Greece and Asia Minor in the same way as wealthy Englishmen of the sixteenth and seventeenth centuries travelled in France and Italy to finish their education. In later days there were missionaries carrying the new Christian faith along the Roman roads, without which, humanly speaking, that faith could not have spread so quickly.

There were several kinds of conveyances in common use. In Rome itself wheeled traffic was not permitted in the daytime, and the litter was much used. This can be described as a kind of couch with a canopy and side-curtains, borne on poles by at least two carriers, and sometimes by as many as six or eight. A kind of sedan chair was sometimes used.

Outside the towns people used the *carpentum*, a light two-wheeled covered cart, drawn by two mules or Gallic horses which were specially prized for their speed. For long journeys travellers used the *raeda*, a four-wheeled carriage that could convey luggage and other personal belongings.

To meet the needs of these mixed crowds of travellers there were inns by the roadside. They were known by their signs as in later times—*Ad Rotam*, The Wheel (which remained throughout the Middle Ages a popular sign for hostelries); *Ad Gallum*, the Cock; or *Ad Dracones*, The Serpents. Outside Rome, on the Appian Way, there was a cluster of inns, the well-known posting station of *Tres Tabernae*, where Paul was met by friends from Rome as he approached the City (Acts xxviii. 15). These taverns, noisy, comfortless, and cheap, were used by humble travellers. There is an inscription which gives a scale of charges under the early Empire. Bread and wine cost one *as* (about ½*d*.) each, and two *asses* were charged for the provender of a mule. At this rate the Good Samaritan made ample provision when he gave the inn-keeper two 'pence' (*denarii*) for the man he befriended. Wealthy men arranged the stages of their journeys so as to stay the night in the houses of friends. Cicero had six houses not far from Rome that he could use in this way. If he could not arrange for the hospitality of friends, a traveller might sleep in his carriage, which was usually large and built for comfort rather than speed. Public officials when travelling were billeted in the houses of leading families. Members of guilds or professional men might often rely on finding hospitality in the house of one of the same guild or profession.

So far we have dealt only with travel by land, chiefly because it was infinitely more popular than travel by sea. The peoples of the ancient world as a whole never fully overcame their fear of the sea. Their point of view can be seen

A Roman magistrate riding in state in a carriage drawn by two horses.
Behind are four men carrying a litter (*lectica*) on their shoulders

A Roman 'coach', a covered four-wheeled vehicle drawn by a pair
of horses

TRAVEL BY LAND

in the lines of Horace where he says that the first man to venture out in his frail craft must have had a heart of oak bound with triple brass. Land journeys were preferred to sea-passages, and from mid-November to the end of March there was little sea traffic; Paul's famous and disastrous journey was made after the usual season was over. There

A merchant ship in the time of the Roman empire

were no ships carrying passengers only; all seafarers had to use merchant ships for their travels. Horace tells us that all parts of the world were visited by merchant ships. A regular service of ships carried grain from Egypt to Rome. All these might be used by travellers at need. We remember that when the centurion brought Paul to Rome he took advantage of 'a ship of Alexandria sailing into Italy' which he found at Myra in Asia Minor.

During the last century of the Republic travel was not always safe. The man who fell among thieves on his way from Jerusalem to Jericho would be a familiar figure to the people who heard the parable. Brigands and robbers on land,

and pirates on the sea, took toll of travellers, as tombstones tell only too frequently, though more commonly the victims were sold into slavery. Robbers had good chances of success because people often preferred to travel by night. The danger was greatly reduced when a strong central government was set up after the Civil Wars of the first century B.C. Pompey cleared the seas of pirates in the year 67, and Augustus established military police posts to give safety on the roads.

XII

THE ROMAN CALENDAR

THE Julian calendar was one of the great gifts of Rome to the world. As its name suggests, it was devised by Julius Caesar. There had been calendars in use before his time, but they were hopelessly inaccurate and had been actually falsified so often that at the time when the reform was made in 46 B.C. the seasons were nearly two months late.

The earliest calendar, said to have been drawn up by Romulus, divided the year into ten months, the first of which was March. Thus September was actually the seventh month (Latin *septem* = seven) and December the tenth month (Latin *decem* = ten). The tradition of a ten-month year cannot be explained satisfactorily. What is certain is that the months were measured by the moon and that during the Republic the years consisted of 355 days, i.e. ten days too few.

To rectify this defect an additional month was inserted from time to time by the priests who controlled the calendar. The result was that at an early date the months ceased to correspond to the phases of the moon, and the calendar fell into confusion.

When Julius Caesar became dictator the reform of the

calendar was a matter of pressing urgency. The seasons were so far out that Cicero, writing once in May, could speak of being delayed by the equinoctial gales. These occur at the end of March, so that the calendar was about six weeks wrong. The intricate calculation needed to correct the calendar was a task after Caesar's heart, for he was well versed in mathematics and astronomy; and it says much for his genius that the alterations he made have stood the test of nearly 2,000 years, with only minor corrections.

Caesar calculated the length of the year as 365¼ days, divided into twelve months. The odd quarter of a day in the Julian reckoning was accounted for once in every four years by the addition of an extra day, as in our leap-year. Caesar put this extra day in February (as we still do), but he arranged for the repetition of the 24th day of the month. Now this, according to the Roman reckoning, was the sixth day before the Kalends of March; so the leap-year was called *Annus Bissextus* (from *bis* = twice, and *sextus* = sixth).

When Julius Caesar set about reforming the calendar, he found that the months and seasons could be brought into their correct relation only by the addition of extra days. Accordingly two additional months were put in between November and December of the year 46 B.C., giving this year a total of 445 days. This extraordinary year has been rightly named *Annus Confusionis*, but with the beginning of the new order of things on the Kalends of January, 45 B.C., the confusion was at an end for good.

It was fitting that this great reform should be commemorated by the giving of its author's name to one of the months. *Quintilis*, at one time the fifth month but now the seventh, was renamed *Julius* in Caesar's honour, and from this we derive the name July. Similarly the next month, *Sextilis*, was renamed *Augustus* (whence August) in honour of Augustus

Caesar. The first six months of the Julian year kept their original names, some of them being derived from the names of the deities to whom those months were sacred. In January (formerly the eleventh month) came the chief festival of the important god Janus; *Februarius* was the month of ceremonial purification, taking its name from *februare*, to cleanse. *Martius* was the month of Mars. *Aprilis*, connected with the verb *aperire* (to open), was the month of unfolding leaves and flowers. *Maius* was sacred to Maia, the genial goddess of summer warmth; and Juno was the deity of the month *Junius*. We have noted already that the months from September to December kept their original names, though these had lost their earlier meaning.

In each month there were three important days to which all the others were counted. These were the *Kalends* (from which we derive our word 'calendar'), *Nones*, and *Ides*, which fell on the first, fifth, and thirteenth days respectively except that

> March, July, October, May
> Make Nones the seventh, Ides the fifteenth day.

The calculation of the dates seems unnecessarily complicated, but it was typical of the cumbersome ways of Roman reckoning. Any given date was counted as being so many days before the Kalends, Nones, or Ides next following, and the day itself was included in the reckoning. Thus, the 24th February, to which reference has been made already, is only five days before the 1st March according to our ideas, but the Romans reckoned it as six. There is a similar idea of inclusive reckoning behind the modern French term for a fortnight—'quinze jours', literally fifteen days; and the Scottish idiom for 'a week hence'—'this day eight days'.

The Romans did not use the seven-day week, which was of Jewish origin, till after Christianity became the official religion of the Empire. Up to that time the Roman week contained eight days—seven ordinary working days and an eighth (called *nundina*[1]) when markets were held.

The days themselves were divided into two main groups—the *Dies Fasti* and *Nefasti*; which were in turn further subdivided. The Dies Fasti took their name from *fas*, that which is binding or obligatory in a moral sense, as used in the famous motto of the Royal Artillery—'Quo Fas et Gloria Ducunt'. It will be seen that the Dies Fasti had a religious importance in the first instance. The Dies Fasti were days on which ceremonial sacrifices, religious banquets, public games, and holidays might take place. The law-courts were open, and the public assemblies of the people were held on the Dies Fasti. Hence by a transference of meaning the word 'Fasti' by itself meant a table or book of all the days of the year with their festivals indicated, after the fashion of a modern calendar.

The Dies Nefasti were the exact contrary of the Fasti. On them no public business might be transacted. They were unlucky days, being very often the anniversary of some disastrous event.

XIII

THE ROMAN ARMY: RANKS AND ORGANIZATION

FOR six and a half centuries of Roman history, service in the army was one of the duties of citizenship, but at the beginning of the first century B.C. a change was made so that from then military service was a means of livelihood.

In the earliest days the army consisted of three legions of

---

[1] See Chapter V. This word is derived from *novem dies*, 'nine days', and is another example of inclusive reckoning.

1,000 men each. The Latin word for a soldier, *miles*, is connected with *mille*, a thousand. One legion was recruited from each of the three tribes in the city, and each legion had a detachment of one hundred horse-soldiers.

Servius Tullius, the sixth king of Rome (578–535 B.C.), made great changes in the organization of the army. Till his reign it had been filled with patricians, but now he made all citizens liable to serve. The people were divided into five classes according to their means, the richest serving as cavalry, the next richest as heavy-armed infantry, and so on downwards to the poorest, who were used as light-armed skirmishers. The humblest of all, who were not included in any of these five classes, were called upon only in times of national peril. There were now four legions of infantry, with cavalry in addition. They fought in the solid formation known as the phalanx with a frontage of five hundred men and six ranks deep.

The phalanx was found to be a somewhat clumsy formation, and by the middle of the fourth century B.C. the legions were divided into 'maniples' (from *manipulus*, a 'handful'), arranged in three groups according to experience. At this period the legion usually contained about 4,200 men, of whom 1,200 were light-armed skirmishers drawn from the poorest classes. The skirmishers entered action first and prepared the way for the men of the first line, known as *hastati*, the young soldiers, who were armed with a spear (*hasta*) for thrusting and a sword for close fighting. If necessary, the second line, the *principes*, more experienced men, were called into action, and if by unlucky chance they were defeated there still remained the third line in reserve, the *triarii*, the oldest and most experienced fighters. This systematic formation remained up to the time of Marius, who completely reorganized the army.

The need for reorganization arose from two causes. First, the campaigns of Rome now took her armies into the farther parts of Europe, and the Near East. No longer could campaigns be finished in a single season as in the old days of wars in Italy; it was no longer possible for a man to do his period of service and then return to his farm or workshop to pick up once more his regular occupation. Secondly, the long wars, and the grievous losses that the Romans suffered both in lives and wealth, had brought about a serious decrease in the number of citizens who were liable to serve in the army under the old system.

Influenced by these two considerations, Marius threw open the army to all who were willing to serve in return for payment. There followed an immense and far-reaching change. Men now adopted the army as a profession, to which they pledged themselves for a period of fifteen to twenty years. They made their oath of allegiance to the general in person, who thereby had at his command a body of paid followers. They were entirely dependent on him and he could, if he wished, use them to further his own purposes rather than those of the State. In this power, of course, lay a great danger.

Marius changed not only the character of the army but also its organization. The old method of grouping the men according to their experience was dropped, though the names of the groups continued in use. The spear had already been replaced by the javelin as the characteristic weapon of the legionary. But perhaps the most important change was the new division of the legion into ten cohorts, each containing three maniples each of which was in turn divided into two centuries. As a century contained roughly one hundred men, a legion at full strength would number about 6,000; in actual practice, however, 5,000 was the usual number. From the time of Marius, the cavalry was made up of foreigners, especially Spaniards and Gauls.

The commander-in-chief was known as the *imperator*. This was simply a title and did not carry any special rank. Originally the army was led by the king himself, and afterwards by the consuls or other magistrates to whom belonged the military command (*imperium*) formerly held by the king.

Each legion in Caesar's army was commanded by a *legatus*, corresponding to a lieutenant-general of to-day—i.e. he was a staff officer who acted for the general in the command of the legion. There were also six tribunes (*tribuni militum*) for each legion. They were appointed by the people as a whole and they held office for one year. A tribune was usually a young man of noble rank.

The *legatus* and the tribunes were the higher officers, of commissioned rank, but the centurions formed the backbone of the legion. There were sixty of them, six in each of the ten cohorts, and they corresponded to the sergeants of a modern army. They were not all of the same standing. In each cohort there were six grades,[1] and the centurions of the first cohort were superior to those of all the other nine cohorts. The ambition of every centurion was to reach the coveted rank of *primus pilus*, the senior centurion of the first cohort, and, therefore, of the whole legion. The system of promotions is not quite clear, but probably a centurion passed from a lower to a higher cohort, keeping the same grade in each. For example, a man holding the rank of *princeps prior* in the sixth cohort would be promoted *princeps prior* in the fifth, and so on till he came to the first cohort. Then he might go from grade to grade till he became *primus pilus*.

[1] The six grades were named from the old divisions of *hastati, principes*, and *pilani* (or *triarii*). They were called *pilus prior* and *posterior, princeps prior* and *posterior*, and *hastatus prior* and *posterior*, the adjectives referring to the front and rear ranks.

The centurions had considerable responsibility and power. Julius Caesar himself regarded his centurions as the men chiefly responsible for controlling the rank and file and for enforcing discipline. We can judge this from his calling together all the centurions after a mutiny in 58 B.C., to rebuke them for not maintaining stricter discipline. Centurions had the right of flogging their men. This was symbolized by carrying a rod which was the special mark of their rank. The brutality of the centurions became proverbial, and the soldiers complained that they had to bribe the centurions to avoid flogging. They used as well to bribe them in order to be let off fatigue duties which were allotted by the centurions. The practice became so common that the officers actually counted on the bribes as a part of their income.

The uniform of a legionary was plain and serviceable. Over a woollen tunic reaching nearly to his knees, he wore a leather doublet with the additional protection of plates of metal if he could afford them. He had a brown-coloured cloak which seems to have been adopted from the Gauls. It could be used as a blanket when required. He wore heavy hobnailed sandals, but no covering to his legs except during campaigns in cold countries like Gaul or Britain, when he might wear puttees or breeches. He was always clean-shaven and wore his hair cut very short.

When in action, he had for defence a crested helmet (first of leather and later of metal) and a leather shield (*scutum*), four feet long and two and a half feet wide, curved almost to the shape of a half cylinder. It was strengthened by a rim of metal and an iron or bronze boss in the middle. The right leg, left uncovered by the shield, was protected by a metal greave; similarly, the right shoulder was protected by a metal disc.

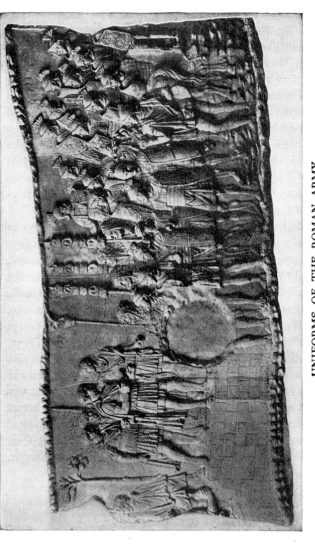

UNIFORMS OF THE ROMAN ARMY

A relief from Trajan's column at Rome representing a general addressing his troops on active service. In front are the standard bearers, behind them the legionaries, and at the back the cavalry

The legionary's weapons were a sword, a javelin, and sometimes a dagger. The sword was short and broad, about two feet in length, two-edged and suitable for hand-to-hand fighting. He carried two javelins for hurling at the enemy in a charge. They were about seven feet long, the shaft being made of wood, with a head (about 2 ft. long) of iron. There was always the danger that these javelins would be picked up and hurled back at the Romans by their enemies; so various means were employed to prevent this. Marius joined the metal point to the shaft with a wooden pin that snapped when the javelin struck, and so the head was loosened; while Julius Caesar made the head (all but the point) of soft iron that bent with the force of a blow.

The legionary had a fair amount of equipment to carry in addition to his personal weapons. It was usually made into a bundle or pack and strapped on to a wooden framework, invented by Marius, that distributed the weight evenly on the shoulders after the fashion of a modern Norwegian ruck-sack. He had to carry, in addition to his personal gear and clothing, entrenching tools and stakes for making the palisade at camp, utensils for cooking his own food, and rations for several days. The bulk of his food was wheat, which was issued to him unground. He had to grind it in his own hand-mill and make his own bread or porridge with it. This ration of grain was counted as part of his wages—he received very little actual cash. Sometimes, as a punishment, barley was issued instead of wheat. The soldiers were not given ordinary wine; their usual drink was a very sour variety, not unlike vinegar. (See St. Mark xv. 36.)

A ROMAN TRANSPORT WAGON

XIV

THE ROMAN ARMY IN THE FIELD

In the last chapter we saw something of the composition of the Roman army; let us now turn to the more important

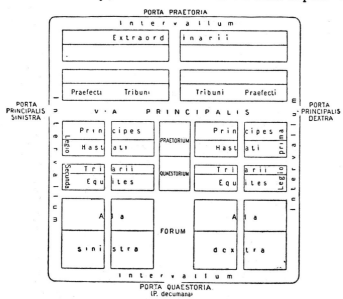

PLAN OF A ROMAN CAMP

topic of the Roman army in the field—on the march, in camp, and engaged in battle or conducting a siege.

There were several ways in which a general might arrange his legions when on the march, the choice depending on the nature of the country through which the army was passing, the nearness of the enemy, the danger of attack, and other considerations. There was always a good deal of baggage (*impedimenta*) to be taken, apart from the soldiers' personal equipment, and this would have to be made safe from attack. The usual arrangement was for each legion to march with its baggage-train immediately following it, protected in the rear (and sometimes on the flanks as well) by the cavalry. The ordinary line of march (*agmen*) was formed in this way, but it was not suitable if there was any immediate danger of meeting the enemy. On such an occasion, several legions went first, followed by all their baggage, with the rest of the army forming a rearguard. Sometimes, when the enemy hovered near with the intention of attacking the flanks of the army, the baggage train was protected by a column of troops on either side, making the formation a hollow square with the baggage in the middle.

When the day's march was finished, normally a distance between fifteen and twenty miles, the army encamped for the night.

A Roman camp (*castra*) was always laid out with the greatest exactness, according to some recognized plan. The one given in the accompanying diagram shows a typical camp of Julius Caesar. The labour involved must have been enormous; but the Romans had that type of genius which finds nothing too much trouble, and of all Roman generals this is perhaps most true of Julius Caesar.

It will be seen that the camp was entirely enclosed by a ditch. The earth removed in the course of digging this was piled up to form a rampart, topped with a palisade. For making this, every legionary carried as many as seven stakes as part of his marching kit. The first point marked by the surveyors who laid out the camp was the site of the general's tent (*praetorium*) which marked the exact middle of the camp. It stood at the junction of the two main thorough-fares that crossed from north to south and from east to west.

There was a gate at the end of each thoroughfare—the main entrance being the Porta Praetoria that was used by the general, and (in theory if not always in fact) was on the eastern side of the camp.

The camp shown in the plan was constructed for two legions and their auxiliaries. Each legion was encamped by itself, one on the south and one on the north of the general's tent. The two encampments were separated by the *forum*; that was the real centre of the life of the camp. Here the general harangued his men; rewards and punishments were meted out; booty was put up for auction; and booths were set up where the soldiers might buy little extras, as in a modern canteen.

As we have seen already, the praetorium formed the general's quarters. It was much more than a mere tent: in a standing camp, indeed, it was a substantial building. In the praetorium were stored the standards and the treasury of the legions. A part of it was set aside for religious uses, especially for the taking of auspices. It contained the quarters of young aristocrats who accompanied the general on his campaigns to gain first-hand practical experience. The *quaestorium* near by formed the quarters of the paymaster, and it was used to house hostages, prisoners, and booty.

The camp was carefully guarded both by day and by night, the hours of darkness being divided into four watches. Pickets of horse and foot were placed at each gate, and sentinels drawn from the light-armed troops mounted guard on the earthmound just inside the surrounding ditch. The watchword (*signum*) was not given by word of mouth, but was written down on wooden tablets, that were passed from man to man throughout the camp from the outer edge inwards to the tribune on duty.

ROMAN LEGIONARY SOLDIERS BUILDING THEIR CAMP

The men who are working all have their helmets off. At the back three officers are superintending the work. On the left is a wood, and the shield of a sentry can be seen. A relief from Trajan's column at Rome

As the order of march varied to suit the circumstances of the occasion, so also the line of battle (*acies*) might be arranged in various ways. The formation used ordinarily by Julius Caesar was known as the *triplex acies*. In this, the ten cohorts of a legion were drawn up in three lines—four in the first line, three in the second line covering the spaces of the first, and three more in the last line. This last line was kept in reserve, and used only if the first two failed in their attack. The four cohorts of the front line, ranged eight deep as a general rule, charged first, hurling their javelins and then engaging the enemy in hand-to-hand fighting with their swords. If necessary the three cohorts of the second line came up to help them, passing through the spaces in the first line. Thus the two front lines shared the attack, resting by turns in order to prepare themselves for any renewal of the fray. The cavalry supported them on the flanks or did battle with the enemy's skirmishers and horsemen, though Roman cavalry did not play a prominent part in actual battles: they were of use chiefly in the pursuit of fugitives.

When a Roman general planned to take a town, he preferred to do so by assault rather than by the slower method of a blockade, and many ingenious machines were brought into use when an assault was made. Sometimes a weakly defended town might be taken by storm. Then the soldiers locked their shields together over their heads as a protection from missiles. Thus they marched to the walls of the town under a roof of shields which was called by the Romans '*testudo*'—the tortoise-shell. As the men under the 'shell' advanced others attempted to scale the walls by means of ladders.

In the capture of stronger towns very elaborate engines of war were employed. Huge earthworks were first con-

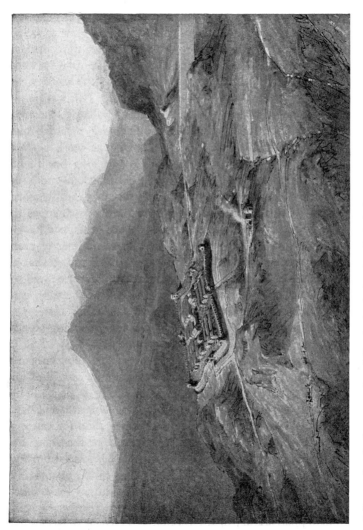

A Roman fort in the mountains of Cumberland, showing the buildings as they originally appeared. Above the fort is Scafell

structed near the walls so that the attackers might meet the defenders on the same level. There were also great wheeled towers, with staging at different heights, that were pushed close to the walls. From these darts and other missiles were hurled against the defenders within, while the walls were weakened with the blows of a battering-ram. This was sometimes just a great beam thrust against the walls by a number of strong men, and sometimes an elaborate machine like that described by Josephus, who saw it at work against the walls of Jerusalem. 'The ram is a vast long beam', he wrote, 'like the mast of a ship, strengthened at one end with a head of iron, something resembling that of a ram, whence it took its name. This is hung by the midst with ropes to another beam, which lies across a couple of posts, and hanging thus equally balanced, it is by a great number of men violently thrust forward and drawn backward, and so shakes the wall with its iron head. Nor is there any tower or wall so thick or strong, that, after the first assault of the ram, can afterwards resist its force in the repeated assaults.' Attempts were also made to dismantle the walls by wrenching stones from them with the help of great iron hooks.

Of course, the Romans had no artillery in the modern sense of the term, but they used various ingenious machines for hurling boulders and other missiles during a siege. The general name given to these machines was *tormenta*, and they were more useful for harassing the enemy than for causing great destruction. The most important were the *catapulta* for discharging darts and arrows, and the *ballista* for hurling stones or beams of timber. The schoolboy to-day shoots tiny pellets in the same way as the Romans hurled their darts against the enemy; so his little implement (really a special kind of bow) is still called a 'catapult'. The *ballista* resembled the mortar of later times. It was worked in the same way as a *catapulta*, but the missile was given its direction by being shot along a groove set at an angle of 45° to the ground.

XV

THE ROMAN ARMY IN TRIUMPH

THE highest ambition of every Roman general was to receive the honour of a Triumph. Yet so strict were the conditions that must be fulfilled before the Senate would grant the honour, that a full Triumph was not often obtained—at least under the Republic. These were the necessary conditions: the victorious general must be either Dictator, or Consul, or Praetor (Pompey was the only exception to this rule); the victory must have been gained in person, and so completely that troops to grace the Triumph might safely be withdrawn from the conquered region; at least five thousand of the enemy must have fallen in battle; and a definite tract of new territory must have been brought under Roman rule.

A Triumph must have been one of the most magnificent of spectacles ever staged in a great city that knew how to make the most of public pageants. On the day when it was held, the whole city made holiday: the streets were decorated with garlands, the statues were adorned with flowers, and fires were lighted on every altar.

The triumphal procession entered the city from the Campus Martius, where the victorious general camped on the preceding night. No effort was spared to glorify the event. First in the long procession came the city magistrates, whose powers were for that day in the hands of the triumphant general. Then followed trumpeters, sounding as for a charge. Next came the spoils taken from the enemy, drawn on chariots or carried by hand, together with representations of the events of the campaign, the places captured, and allegorical figures, all mounted upon stages set upon wagons, as we see *tableaux vivants* in a Lord Mayor's Show to-day. White oxen intended for sacrifice came next, adorned very richly, led by priests and followed by others bearing the sacred vessels and implements of sacrifice. After that came the captives, headed by the king of the conquered country, his children, and his chief nobles. If it chanced that the king had fallen in battle, his effigy was carried in the procession. Then followed officials of the victorious army, and musicians dancing and playing.

Next was the general himself in whose honour the whole wonderful pageant was taking place. He was drawn in a rich circular chariot by four horses, always, from the time of Julius Caesar, pure white. He was robed in purple and wore a laurel crown. In his right hand he carried a laurel branch, and in his left an ivory sceptre. Behind him stood a slave, holding above the victor's head the crown of Jupiter in the form of an oak-wreath made of gold: and sometimes, curiously enough, another slave to whisper reminders that he was but human, lest he should become too proud with the honours heaped upon him. With the general in his chariot were his children if they were very young; if they were lads who had not yet assumed the *toga virilis*, they rode on the horses that drew the chariot; if grown up they rode behind, with the *legati* and *tribuni* of the victorious army. Last of all came the soldiers, marching on foot, their javelins twined with laurel, shouting *Io triumphe* and singing songs in honour of their general.

The immense procession entered the city by a special gate, the *Porta Triumphalis*, which was used only on these occasions. On the line of route, triumphal arches were erected, at one time as occasion required but afterwards built permanently of stone, often elaborately decorated. Some still remain, and others like them may be seen in Paris, commemorating the victories of Napoleon. The procession passed through the Circus Maximus and along the Sacred Way to the Forum, whence the general ascended the Capitoline Hill to the great Temple of Jupiter. While he mounted thither, and as an integral part of the day's events, the principal captives were put to death in a prison adjoining the Forum: it is recorded that only on four occasions were their lives spared. Upon entering the Temple of Jupiter, where the white oxen were sacrificed, the general laid his laurel branch upon the lap of the god. The sacrifices were followed by a state banquet given by the Senate, and feasts for the soldiers and citizens.

Even when the day's pageant was over, the general enjoyed further honours of victory. He still wore his laurel wreath. He received land to build a house, the entrance to which was decorated with his trophies, while his statue in a triumphant chariot was placed in the entrance hall to keep his memory green. Even after his death his triumph was not forgotten, for his ashes were allowed burial within the walls of the city.

If the Romans wished to honour a general not entitled to a full Triumph, they gave him an Ovation. This also was a procession through the streets, but shorn of the splendours of a Triumph. The general entered the city on foot, or (in later times) on horseback, clad in the ordinary toga of a magistrate. Instead of the laurel wreath, he wore one of myrtle, and he carried no sceptre. There were neither troops nor magistrates in the procession, but usually some *equites* and a throng of the humbler citizens. Music was provided by flutes, instead of by the trumpets of war. And when the procession reached the Temple of Jupiter, instead of white oxen, a sheep was sacrificed. The honour of an ovation was granted when the enemy was not very dangerous, or when the bloodshed had not been considerable.

Awards to individual soldiers for bravery or for specially good service in the field commonly took the form of crowns; and it was a general principle that the greatest honour was attached to the crowns that were the least valuable in themselves. So to-day the Victoria Cross, in our own army the highest award for valour, is merely an inexpensive medal of bronze. Its Roman equivalent was the civic crown (*corona civica*), that was awarded to soldiers who saved the lives of Roman citizens in battle. It was made simply of oak leaves. Special honours were paid to holders of the civic crown: when they entered a public building, all those present rose to show their respect; and they had the right to sit with Senators at public entertainments. Other crowns of different designs were awarded for special kinds of distinguished service in action. Various trophies in the form of collars, bracelets, and horse-trappings were conferred when a crown was not an appropriate reward. There were many awards and they were lavishly bestowed, but the Romans aimed at encouraging valour and zeal so that cowardice and slackness might but rarely show themselves.

XVI

NAVAL AFFAIRS

IN all the long and wonderful story of Rome, few incidents show the fine spirit of the Romans better than the building of their first fleet when war broke out with Carthage (B.C. 264). Up to that time the Romans had had very little to do with the sea; and their only vessels were clumsy merchant-ships. Carthage, on the other hand, was the greatest naval power in the ancient world, and Rome had to prepare to meet her in naval conflict.

By a fortunate chance a Carthaginian galley was stranded on the Italian coast. The Romans took this for their model

A ROMAN BATTLESHIP
being rowed into action, with a detachment of soldiers on board

and set about building a fleet. So that there should be no delay in putting to sea when the ships were built, the crews were made to practise rowing on benches set up on dry land, in much the same way as we can practise swimming exercises out of the water to-day. With the fleet that came into being in this way the Romans were able to defeat the Carthaginians.

True, the story of the stranded Carthaginian ship is open to doubt. For a long time before the wars with Carthage the Romans had been obliged to turn their attention to the sea, in the course of their dealings with the Greeks of Southern

Italy, from whom they could always recruit trained sailors. The Romans must have been familiar with Etruscan and Greek vessels, and it is noteworthy that their earliest coins bore the prow of a ship on one side. It is quite likely that Roman historians purposely overlooked these facts in their desire to enhance the glory of their triumph over Carthage.

But the Romans did not extend their naval power—they were still afraid of the sea. It has been thought that the Romans kept no standing navy, but preferred to build ships as and when necessity arose. This was not often, for most campaigns were conducted by land; but when sea travel was necessary, as when Julius Caesar came to Britain, lack of experience often brought mishap or disaster. Those vessels they had were always hauled up on to the shore at the end of the autumn, and were not launched again till the early summer.

The general name for a warship was *navis longa*. It was comparatively narrow for its length, being designed mainly for speed, unlike the merchant ship that needed plenty of space for its cargo. The 'long-ships' were propelled by oars, and the different kinds were named biremes, triremes, quadriremes, quinqueremes, and so on (from *remus*, an oar). At one time it was thought that these names implied the number of the banks of oars on the various ships, but it is now believed that they show the number of rowers to each oar: thus, there would be three rowers to each oar on a trireme, and five on a quinquereme, the two commonest types of boat in use.

The rowers were seldom, if ever, of Roman birth. Usually they came from allied or conquered races, or were slaves who had gained their freedom. They formed the crew and were quite separate from the fighting men, who in the early days were ordinary legionaries, but later were specially recruited for service in the fleet after the manner of our Royal Marines.

The officers on each ship were the Master (*Magister*) and the steersman (*gubernator*), though sometimes one man filled both offices.

In a naval engagement, three methods of attack might be used. First, the attacker might crash its way through the oars of the enemy's ship and so leave it disabled. Or, by skilful steering, one ship might ram another with its bronze-shod 'beak' (*rostrum*), level with or below the surface of the water. If neither of these tactics succeeded, two vessels would manœuvre alongside each other. Then, when they had been linked with grappling-irons, boarding planks would be laid across from one to the other and close hand-to-hand fighting on the decks would follow.

XVII

THE RELIGION OF THE ROMANS

In order to understand fully the ideas that underlay the religion of the Romans, we must go back to the earliest days of the Latin settlements in Italy. The newcomers were tillers of the soil, and their daily work brought them into ceaseless struggle with the forces of Nature. There were many things that these primitive people experienced but could not explain. Floods and drought, storms and refreshing showers, untimely frosts and genial summer warmth were at work to bring them either good fortune or disaster.

In all these everyday happenings they saw the work of spirits, sometimes hurtful and at other times beneficent. At every turn they believed themselves to be surrounded by spirits (*numina*), in air, in earth and water—spirits that could help or harm them, always resenting any encroachment, always ready to smite the trespasser, yet equally ready to favour and assist if won over by acceptable sacrifices and ceremonies. Where there was so much that could not be explained, ignorance bred superstition, which in turn gave rise to fear; so that the whole purpose of 'religion' was to secure the favour of the spirits, or to make amends to any and every deity (*numen*) that might be offended in the course of a man's everyday occupations. If a man bridged a stream, for instance, even if it were only with a plank, he must make sacrifice to the river-spirit for intruding upon his domain. In this deep-rooted belief in spirits we find the foundations of Roman religion. There was in it an element of magic, and a belief that certain acts would produce certain results that were to be desired or avoid others that were to be feared. So among the Romans there were magical ceremonies for making rain, as there are in West Africa to-day, and such ceremonies continued to be used, with certain changes, right on into the historical period of Roman history when the people had outgrown the days of magic.

Yet though the basis of the religion of the early Romans was this belief in spirits, the people had only the most shadowy notions about them. They had not enough imagination to give them a form, a physical shape. The gods remained as spirits, often merely described by an adjective indicating the qualities or dwelling of the spirit, as Silvanus, the god of the wild wood (*silva*). Sometimes the idea was carried a stage farther and it was believed that a particular spirit dwelt in a certain place or thing. Thus the god Terminus dwelt in his stone on the Capitol; Diana in her grove at Aricia, and Volturnus in the River Tiber. It is most important to remember that the early Romans had only vague ideas to work upon; for we find that they were accustomed to add various qualities to these shadowy spirits. We may take as an example the great god Jupiter who was worshipped under many different titles: e.g. Jupiter Stator, the stayer of flight in war, or Jupiter Ruminus who fertilized the earth with rain. It must be remembered that the Romans did not attempt to represent Jupiter or their other early gods in any special physical form. Centuries later, when they came into contact with the Greeks, they discovered amongst the Greek gods and goddesses many that were counterparts of their own, and they

A grove on a hill-top near Rome, sacred in Roman times. Such groves were often looked upon by the Romans as the haunt of some special god or goddess

copied the Greeks in making images, often in human form, though in the early days their ideas had been so vague that they did not know whether to address the spirits as god or goddess.

To see the religion of the Romans at its best and purest, unchanged by contact with foreign practices and beliefs, we must go to the private religion of the family, from which the State religion developed. Family ties were very strong, and one of the strongest was the religion of the household, that centred round the things of everyday life. There was the worship of the spirit of the door, Janus (from *ianua*), who guarded the entrance to the home and looked after all who went out or came in. Within the house there was the spirit of the hearth-fire, Vesta. Indoors there were as well the Penates, the spirits of the store-cupboard (*penus*). Very important, too, was the worship of the Genius of the family, though the underlying idea is rather difficult to understand nowadays. It was that indefinable something that makes every family different from all others. The Genius was in some way connected with the head of the family. Thus, for example, its festival was observed on the master's birthday; and when the Romans gave their deities an individual physical form, they represented the Genius in the likeness of the head of the family. The family religion also included the worship of the Lares.[1] They were probably gods of the fields before being brought indoors, for Cicero tells us they were worshipped in sight of the house. The family shrine, the *Lararium*, was set up in the atrium, showing how intimately the Lar was connected with the daily life of the family. In the early days, when life was more simple, these family deities would be worshipped by the sacrifice of a part of the meal that was thrown into the flames; in later days the images of Lares and Penates were placed upon the table to show that they had a share in the meal. Even in more luxurious times, there was a pause in every banquet while offerings were taken to the household gods. It was only natural that in the family religion the head of the family should be the priest, a fact which emphasized his importance and formed a strong bond between members of the family.

But families did not live apart. They were from very early times grouped in clans or tribes living together in country districts. Naturally they had religious rites and ceremonies that must be performed in common. These festivals were connected with the important seasons of the farmer's year—

[1] See Chapter III.

the spring-time, harvest, and winter. In early times the Roman year began in March,[1] the beginning of the Spring period of growth. There came a lull in the activity of the farm during June and July, and not till the harvest months of August and October do we find more great agricultural festivals. The winter festivals, of which the chief was the Saturnalia, were connected with the preparations for the next year's crops.

It was from the religion of the farm and the family that the Roman State religion grew up.

In the first place we must notice that some of the chief gods of the City-State had their origin in the gods of the household. There was Vesta, whose undying fire guarded by the Vestal Virgins represented the continuous life of the city as in the house it represented the life of the family. In the home the hearth fire was tended by the daughters of the household; so the Vestal Virgins, the guardians of the city fire, were regarded as something like daughters of the Pontifex Maximus, who took the place of the king at the head of the religion of the State. Janus guarded the gateways of the city as he also protected the doorway of the house. And other ideas were associated with this god. Since he watched all who went out and came in he must look both ways: hence he was represented with two heads. He was the god of all beginnings and the 'father of the morning' to whom the first prayer of the day was offered. The city also had its Lares and Penates, fulfilling on a larger scale the duties of the household gods; and in place of the Genius of the family there was the Genius of the Roman people, and of the city itself, and finally of the Emperor, who stood in the same relation to the nation as did the father to the family.

[1] See Chapter XII.

Perhaps the most interesting development was that which changed the vague spirits that watched over the affairs of men into gods with a definite form and traditional legends. The idea came first from the Etruscans, but was chiefly developed through contact with the Greeks, who had more imagination than the Romans. From very early times the Greeks had given a definite form, usually human, to the spirits which they believed were in the world around them. The Romans found that the Greeks had many deities very like their own, and as they were represented in human shapes that could be more easily understood than vague spirits, the Romans copied the Greeks and made statues of their gods.

At first Jupiter was the spirit (or *numen*) who inhabited the sky. From this it was natural that he should become the god of light (with the adjectival title of Lucetius, from *lux*), and should be worshipped at the times of full moon when there was most light both by night and day. He was also the spirit that hurled the thunderbolt; places struck by lightning were sacred to him since he moved in the lightning-flash. Yet he was still a spirit, specially connected with the sacred oak on the Capitoline Hill. When the Romans came back from their early wars bringing their spoils with them, they laid the choicest on this sacred oak; and so Jupiter became connected with successful warfare. As Jupiter Stator he stayed the rout when Roman armies were hard pressed; as Jupiter Victor he gave them triumph; in his temple on the Capitol he was the supreme head of the State, Jupiter Optimus Maximus, the 'best and greatest'. 'To his temple the Roman youth will come to make his offering when he takes the dress of manhood; here the magistrates will do sacrifice before entering their year of office; here the victorious general will pass in procession with the spoils of victory; on the walls shall be suspended treaties with foreign nations and offerings sent by subject princes and states from all quarters of the world: all that Rome is to be, will be, as it were, embodied in the sky-spirit of the sacred oak, the god of justice and of victory in war.'[1]

The same sort of process took place in the thoughts

STATUE OF A VESTAL VIRGIN

Found in tne house of the Vestal Virgins in the Forum at Rome

of the Romans about their great god Mars, though here, curiously enough, it was a complete change rather than a mere development. Mars was a deity worshipped by all the tribes that settled in Latium, but at first he was in chief a god of the fields. We shall see that farmers prayed to Mars for protection of their crops and live stock, and for abundant harvest. Yet to the later Romans Mars was chiefly the grim

[1] C. Bailey.

god of war, whose sacred animal was the fierce wolf. We can trace the reason for this change if we consider the time of the chief festivals of Mars. They fall in March, the month sacred to him, and in May—both of them months of the early year, when the crops were beginning to grow and when the young men were donning their armour in readiness for the summer campaigns. And so in the beginning he was really in two ways the 'spirit of the growing year'—first, as the ally of the farmer in giving increase to his flocks and fields, and second of the warrior who goes seeking the fortunes of war. Of course, at different periods of Roman history, one or other of the sides of his nature would be the more important: in the early days when the Romans were a tribe of farmers, they would think of Mars as a god of the countryside; later on when they became a nation of soldiers they thought of him as the god of war.

As time passed many deities were adopted by the Romans and a distinction arose between the *Di indigetes*, or native gods, and the *Di novensiles*, or new gods. It was only natural that the native gods were those connected directly or indirectly with agriculture, the gods that had been at one time the *numina* of the early settlers.

The newer gods of foreign origin, the *Di novensiles*, came from various countries that the Romans conquered, but especially from Greece. Some were adopted at a very early date—e.g. Minerva, an Etruscan goddess of the arts and crafts, and Diana, who was introduced from Aricia when the Latin league was formed. When a new god was brought from Greece it was usually just a matter of identifying an already existing deity with its Greek counterpart, and assigning to it the stories that the more imaginative Greeks had woven round their more definite god or goddess. Thus we find that

Neptunus, the god of seas and streams, was the Roman counterpart of the Greek Poseidon; Mercurius, a god of trading, was identified with the Greek Hermes, the messenger of the gods. Some of the later gods, it is true, had no real counterpart in early Roman religion. The worship of Phoebus Apollo was almost purely Greek, as also was that of Aesculapius, the god of healing, since the Romans had very little knowledge of medicine. The cult of Isis was imported direct from Egypt, while in 205 B.C. a great fetish rock was brought from Phrygia to be worshipped as the Great Mother (*Magna Mater*).

With all these many and different deities, a Roman's dealings were of a very practical nature. He sought either to avoid their ill will or, more often, to enlist their active support. His prayers were for definite material blessings, and when he offered a sacrifice it was with the idea of getting some benefit in return or of avoiding some evil. Cicero himself points out that a Roman did not pray to be made virtuous, but to be made both healthy and wealthy.

One important reason for this cold attitude towards religion was the Romans' dislike of changes, and their faithful following of the practice of their forefathers (*mos maiorum*). Another reason was the control of religion by the State. It is scarcely too much to say that a man's dealings with the gods were marked out as definitely for him as were his dealings with his fellow citizens.

The close connexion of religion with the State is clearly seen in the organization of the priesthood. Here it should be noted that the priests were not usually trained specially for their duties nor did they form a class apart from other citizens. Indeed, it often happened that men who had distinguished themselves in other departments of public life were appointed to some of the highest priestly offices. Thus the Emperors took the title of Pontifex Maximus, though they did not carry out the duties belonging to the office.

In the earliest days the king presided over religion as one branch of the city's life. When the kingship was abolished and the duties of the kings were divided among a number of individuals, certain orders of priesthood (*collegia*) came into being.

The most important was that of the Pontifices, who practically controlled the State religion. They gave judgement on all religious matters; they had disciplinary powers over the lesser orders of priesthood; they laid down the rules for public worship, for all feasts and sacrifices, and regulated the calendar. In the opinion of Cicero, the honour and safety of the commonwealth, the liberty of the people, the houses and fortunes of the citizens, and even the gods themselves were all entrusted to their care, and depended entirely on their wisdom and judgement. The head of this order, the Pontifex Maximus, was one of the chief men in the city.

The second great order was that of the Augurs, who (together with the Auspices) were concerned with the interpretation of omens, i.e. the prophecy of forthcoming events by observing certain signs. There were at first three augurs, one for each tribe, but their number was increased to fifteen as time passed. Their duty was to interpret dreams and oracles, and to declare whether the omens were good or bad. The interpretations of augurs were mainly concerned with public affairs.

Auspices on the other hand were employed at every turn in connexion with the household, the farm, and the State, whenever any important enterprise was to be undertaken —whether it was a betrothal, a sowing, or a battle. The auspices might be taken by the master of the house, a magistrate,

THE STATE RELIGION OF ROME

A ceremonial procession entering a temple

or a general according to the occasion, but an augur was usually consulted to interpret the signs observed. The derivation of the word auspices (*avis*, *spicere*) shows that the chief signs observed were the actions, and especially the flight, of birds; but the Romans were superstitious and tried to read some meaning into any unusual or special occurrence, even such a thing as a flash of lightning if appearing at certain times.

The whole purpose of augury and auspices was clearly to find out in advance what was the will of the gods; it reveals another plain indication of the Romans' dread of the deities they could not understand and their desire to propitiate them and to win their goodwill and help.

XVIII

FESTIVALS AND SACRIFICES

WE have already seen that the belief in nature-spirits was the basis of Roman religion. Many survivals of it can be seen in the private religion of the family. It also accounts for the special features of the great festivals which otherwise would have had little meaning for people living in a great city.

There were usually two purposes underlying these festivals —first, to appease any numina that might have been offended, and secondly, to put a place, or thing, or person under the protection of the god whose goodwill had been obtained by sacrifice. The appeasing of the numina was known as a *lustratio*, or cleansing from guilt. The whole people and the city were 'purified' in this way at regular intervals, just as were the Israelites by the laws of Moses. More often it was just a single family and its possessions and dependents that were 'purified', and on such occasions it was the head of the family, the paterfamilias, who acted as priest.

The festival known as the Parilia may be taken as revealing most of the characteristic features of Roman festivals. It was in honour of Pales, a very ancient spirit of the countryside, and therefore it takes us back to the early days of the settlement of farmers. The poet Ovid has given us a full account of the festival, with much picturesque detail, so that we can see it all very clearly in imagination. In the early morning the shepherds 'purified' their flocks and swept the ground clean with a broom made of twigs, afterwards decorating the folds with branches. A fire was made of olive-wood, juniper, pine twigs, and laurel, upon which sulphur was thrown. Offerings were made of millet, millet cakes, and a pail of milk warm from the cow to Pales. Prayers were offered to all and any of the spirits that might have been unknowingly offended, and petitions made for freedom from disease and misfortune. A special prayer was then recited four times, those who were taking part in the festival meanwhile turning to the east. Finally there was a twofold act of purification. The worshippers washed their hands in a running stream, and then leaped through fires made of lighted straw. The flocks and herds were also driven through the fires. In this festival of Parilia, we find purification, rustic offerings, and prayers for good fortune and fertility in fields and flocks—all the features of a typical Roman festival. Such festivals were observed, in letter if not always in spirit, long after the Romans had ceased to be a nation of farmers, but they served to remind the people of the old days of magic when they drew their living from the soil.

Another typical and picturesque festival of a similar kind was the Ambarvalia that was celebrated in May, just before the early harvests began. It was a family festival for the purification and protection of the farm lands from the evil spirits that dwelt outside.

All work was laid aside on the day of the festival, while the master and his servants made a procession three times round the fields, leading with them the animals appointed for sacrifice—a pig, a sheep, and an ox, a combination of offerings also used at other times and known as *suovetaurilia*, a compound of *sus*, *ovis*, and *taurus*. The special prayer offered to Mars is of interest because it shows so clearly the whole purpose of the festival. 'Father Mars, I pray and beseech thee that thou mayest be gracious and favourable to me, to my home, and to my household, for which cause I have ordained that the offering of pig, sheep, and ox be carried round my fields, my land, and my farm; that thou mayest avert, ward off, and keep afar all disease, visible and invisible, all barrenness, waste, misfortune, and ill weather; that thou mayest suffer our crops, our corn, our vines and bushes to grow and come to prosperity; that thou mayest preserve the shepherds and the flocks in safety, and grant health and strength to me, to my home, and to my household.'

The procession wound its way round the limits of the farm, with dancing, merry-making, and the singing of chants in honour of Ceres, the goddess of crops. At turning-points in the boundaries turf-built altars were set up, and on them sacrifice was made to the goddess. The head of the family acted as priest on this occasion as on many others. The purpose of the festival was not only to 'purify' the farm and to call upon the aid of Mars and, later, of Ceres, but also to mark the boundaries between the realms of Ceres and those of Silvanus, deities of the tilled and the untilled lands respectively. The Ambarvalia and the lesser festivals of purification of farm-lands were observed with more pious sincerity than most other festivals, since the meaning and purpose of them was still realized by those who took part. Strangely enough we find a survival of a similar idea in our own times. This is

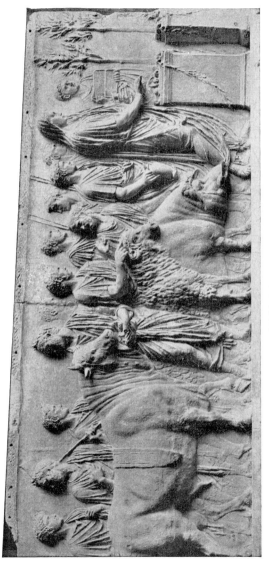

SUOVETAURILIA

The second man from the left carries on his shoulder the axe

the 'beating of the bounds' of a parish, usually in early summer, at Rogation-tide (from the Latin *rogare*, to petition), when a procession goes round the boundaries, halting at certain points, where psalms are sung and a certain amount of horse-play takes place.

Almost every month brought to the Romans one or more festivals connected with agriculture in its many different forms. In August the harvests were gathered in and special festivals marked the happy event. The Consualia was the most important, when the sacrifices made at the underground altar of Consus, the god of the storehouse, were an echo of the primitive custom of storing grain underground. With a touch of feeling unusual in the austere Romans of a later age, they freed from work the beasts of burden that had worked to bring in the harvest as they had also done at the festival of Parilia.

Much of the spirit of our 'harvest home' is to be found in the merry-making of the Saturnalia, the winter festival of the sowing. The festival began on December 17th, and while it lasted social differences were forgotten. Slaves became the equal of their masters, whose guests they were at a feast, in much the same way as Society people of to-day often give a 'servants' ball' at Christmas, when the relative positions of master and servant are reversed for the time being. Many of our Christmas festivities are no more than an adaptation of this pagan festival of the Saturnalia to the use of Christians.

It remains to say something of the rites with which sacrifices were offered. First we must remember that a sacrifice was a bargain made with the deity whose goodwill was sought. Hence it was always necessary that no ceremonial detail should be omitted, that there should be no hitch or untoward mischance to mar the proceedings, or the slightest departure from the strict rules governing the sacrifice. If any such irregularity did occur, it was thought necessary to start again from the beginning. In order to avoid this in the great public ceremonies, it was usual to sacrifice a pig the day before, to make good in advance any mistake or omission.

There were often special ceremonies connected with the worship of individual deities, but the general ordering of a sacrifice was much the same on all occasions. The sacrificial animal (*victima* if a large beast; *hostia* if a sheep or smaller) was led to the slaughter decorated with garlands and white ribbons, or with its horns gilded. In the procession to the altar, a crier went first to warn the people to leave their work and attend the ceremony. Next came musicians with pipes and harps.

Having reached the altar, the priest, who was always robed in white, rested his hand upon it, and first recited a solemn prayer in a low voice, his head being covered lest he should see anything of ill omen. The strictest silence had to be observed by all standing near and the pipers played all the while lest any sound of ill omen should be heard. After the prayer the priest began the ceremony of sacrifice by sprinkling on the head of the beast corn or frankincense mixed with the *mola salsa*, a cake of meal and salt. Then the priest sprinkled wine from a dish on to the head of the beast, after first sipping from the dish himself and then offering it to those who stood near. Next, having plucked some hairs from the head of the beast and thrown them into the fire on the altar, the priest marked the victim with a knife, and handed it over to those whose duty it was to slay it. When the animal was killed, its entrails were carefully removed and the auspices came to inspect them. If anything unusual was found, any blemish, it was necessary to begin again with another beast; but if all was well, the choicest parts of the entrails were sprinkled with meal and wine and incense, and then thrown into the flames on the altar. More solemn prayers were recited, and then the multitude was dismissed with the solemn word *Ilicet* (=*ire*+*licet*). The sacrifice being finished, the priest and his assistants regaled themselves on the flesh of the victim.

XIX

THE GOVERNMENT OF ROME

THE government of Rome in the last century B.C. shows very clearly that the Romans disliked changes and that they clung loyally to the ways of their forefathers (*mores maiorum*). That being so, we must know something of the government of the early city in the days of the kings in order to understand the form of government at the time of Cicero and Julius Caesar. We must also remember that when Rome grew from a small settlement of farmers into a widespread 'empire' containing many different countries and peoples, the Romans tried to adapt the old system of government instead of devising an entirely new one.

In the earliest days of the City-State, the government was entirely in the hands of the king, who ruled the people in very much the same way as the *paterfamilias* ruled the family— that is to say, he was concerned with their welfare in all departments of the life and work of the city. His power, which was supposed to be unlimited and absolute, was called *imperium*, the name used throughout Roman history for the chief power in the State. The king had the power to punish; as a symbol of which bundles of rods, known as *fasces*, were carried by lictors before him and also before the magistrates of later days. (Similarly to-day the mace, which really is only a special kind of hammer, is carried before the mayor, i.e.

the chief magistrate of his city or borough, as a sign of his power to punish.)

The kings of Rome had three main duties. They had to deal with all questions concerning religion, with law and

LAW AND ORDER

A memorial to a Roman magistrate, showing his official chair (which is made to fold up like a camp-stool) and, on either side, the *fasces*

justice, and with warfare. Only in the last was the king's power really unlimited. In all religious matters the king was helped by the priests and by the augurs, about whom we have read in an earlier chapter. In all things concerning law and justice, the king had the advice of the Senate, a council of elderly men, experienced in public affairs, in much the same way as the Saxon kings of England were advised by the Witan, the council of the 'wise men'.

When the kings were driven out at the close of the sixth century B.C., the Romans tried to create a form of government that would involve the fewest possible changes but would at the same time prevent the misrule for which the kings were expelled. In the first place it was decided that no longer was the great power of the *imperium* to be in the hands of one man. It was still regarded as existing, but with this very important difference—it was now in the control of the whole body of the citizens; it had become a public thing (*res publica*); and all those who enjoyed the privilege of being Roman citizens were to have a voice in controlling the power by which they were governed. They had overthrown the kings and they would now control the rulers that took their place. It must always be remembered, however, that the old idea of an *imperium*, or supreme power, was still retained, but it had to be held in check to prevent its being misused.

In the first place, the highest rank in the government was to be held by two men, the consuls, who had equal power. Each could act as a check upon the other so that neither could become tyrannical. They were in office for one year only, during which brief time it would be difficult for them to make themselves too powerful. Moreover, they were elected by the people as a whole in their assemblies, and, like the presidents of most modern republics, when their year of office was ended they became private citizens once more, though they had a place in the Senate and might also be appointed to other public posts. However, the strongest check on the power of the consuls was the Senate, of whom we shall have more to say later in this chapter. Many senators had held some official rank in the government and they were able to give the consuls the benefit of their experience. While the consuls were not compelled by any law to accept the advice of the Senate, they dared not disregard it. Though, as a general rule, the power of the consuls was limited in these various ways, in times of national peril the consuls were allowed, with the approval of the Senate, to appoint a dictator. A dictator held his office for a definitely limited period, but during that time he had unlimited power in all departments of the government and the army.

In addition to the consuls, there were other magistrates who shared some of the former duties and powers of the kings. Of these the praetors, like the consuls, had the full *imperium*. Their duties were to see to the carrying out of the laws and the control of justice. At first there was only one praetor in Rome, but by 242 B.C. so many foreigners were dwelling in the city or came there on business, that in that year a second praetor was appointed. He had to take charge of the legal affairs of foreigners in Rome. The original official was called the *praetor urbanus*; this new one, *praetor peregrinus*. As time went on and the 'empire' grew larger, the amount of legal business increased. To keep pace with this increase, more praetors were appointed, as in England the number of judges has been increased from time to time when need arose. Moreover, as new provinces were added to the Roman world, the governorship of them was often entrusted to praetors of these provinces.

The other important officials in the government of Rome were the censors, the aediles, the quaestors, and the tribunes. None of these had the full power of the *imperium*. Nevertheless, the censors filled a very honoured position in the city, and to be made censor was considered as the successful end of a public career. The censors were appointed for five years, but acted officially for only eighteen months. Their chief duties were—to draw up lists of the citizens and to supervise their conduct and behaviour; and, at the end of their period of office, to carry out a solemn 'purification' of all the people, as we have described in an earlier chapter.

The aediles (who took their name from *aedes*, a house or building) had the oversight of all public works: they were, for instance, responsible for keeping the public buildings in repair, and cleaning the streets. The quaestors were officials who looked after the funds in the public treasury. They often had to go with the consuls when they went to war, to look after the money matters connected with the campaign.

The tribunes had great power, which had come about indirectly, and in the following way. In the very early days there were two classes of citizens, known as patricians and plebeians. The patricians were descended from the families who had made the earliest settlement; the plebeians belonged to the families who had settled in Rome in later times. At first the patricians had all the power of governing the city in their hands. They alone could be appointed to the public posts in the Republic. Yet the plebeians had the chief share in defending the city; so they naturally claimed a share in the government. The patricians would not grant their claim and a quarrel arose which lasted for many years. On one occasion the plebeians actually left Rome and threatened to make a fresh settlement. It was then, in 494 B. C., that the tribunes were first appointed. Their duty was to look after the interests of the plebeians, and of course they were themselves plebeians. They were required to keep a watchful eye on the actions of the Senate and of the magistrates; and if either intended to do anything against the welfare of the plebeians, the tribunes had power to forbid it. This was really a very great power, and used unwisely would hinder progress. However, one tribune could forbid the action of another, and as they did not always agree together, they weakened the power of one another. (It should be noted that by the time that the struggle between the patricians and the plebeians was over, 337 B.C., every part in the government of the city had been thrown open to them. The first plebeian consul was elected in 367 B.C.)

In theory any Roman with full rights of citizenship might be appointed to the highest positions in the government, but in actual fact this privilege was restricted to certain favoured families. They were some of the best of the patricians and the plebeians, and it was quite the usual thing to find that all the near relations of an official had held government appointments before him. It was a bold man who sought to be elected to high office unless he belonged to this charmed circle of those who enjoyed senatorial rank. Cicero was one of the few who succeeded though he belonged to the lower order known as *equites*. At one time they were the class of citizens who provided the cavalry in the army, but by the end of the Republic they were a distinct social class (*ordo*), comprising chiefly the big business-men such as merchants, bankers, and moneylenders.

The magistrates held office for only short periods, as we have seen, lest they should become too powerful. But behind the frequently changing ranks of magistrates, the Senate went on unchanging. The result was that the Senate became more and more powerful, especially during the years when Rome was fighting for her existence against Carthage. Not only was the Senate permanent, but by the last century B.C. it was composed entirely of men who had held office and whose knowledge of affairs was of great value in guiding the State. The Senate was in fact, though not in name, the real government. At first the senators were chosen by the king; then by the consuls, and, still later, by the censors; but from the time of Sulla every man who had served as a quaestor (and that was the first step in a man's public career) automatically became a senator.

Having said this much about the importance of the Senate, we shall not be surprised to find that the senators did a great deal of public work. They made the laws, directly or indirectly. A magistrate usually made sure of their favour before any bill was brought before the assemblies of the citizens. A decree of the Senate (*senatus consultum*) was equal to a law. The Senate controlled the money of the State, in its spending and even in making the coins, for the letters SC on coins showed that they were made by order of the Senate. The senators also dealt with questions concerning the government of the provinces. All matters of peace and war were really settled in the Senate, though the final decision rested with the citizens in their assemblies. In the best days of Rome the Senate was a fine dignified body of eminent citizens, worthy of their great city. No wonder was it that the messengers of the Greek king Pyrrhus described the Senate as an assembly of kings. In later times it became less worthy of honour and respect.

The Senate really did the effective work of government, though in theory this was supposed to rest with the magistrates and the people as a whole who appointed them. The people expressed their wishes in the various assemblies (*comitia*) in which they met together. These assemblies differed only in the way the people voted. It might be by tribes, or by centuries, or by *curiae*—the thirty divisions into which the whole people were grouped in the early days of the city.

The various assemblies were supposed to have the last word in deciding such important matters as the election of the magistrates or questions of peace and war. Actually the Senate made up their minds, and then put the question to the assemblies, who got into the habit of agreeing without

A ROMAN SENATOR

question. If there was likely to be any difficulty, there were various ways (of which bribery was one) by which the lower ranks of citizens could be won over to support any particular measure. Such methods were made all the more easy by the fact that the votes were taken by groups and not individually. When the assemblies agreed to a measure proposed by the Senate it became law (*lex*).

The greatest weakness of the rule of Rome was revealed in the government of the provinces. Misgovernment perhaps would be a better word. When a provincial governor was sent out to his province he had no set of rules for his guidance. He acted as he thought best. If he was a worthy man, well and good, but there were great temptations in the practically unlimited powers of a provincial governor. To hold a magistracy in Rome was a very expensive matter, and many provincial governors looked to pay their debts and make a fortune out of the taxes that could be squeezed from the unfortunate provincial subjects. They held office for only a few years at most and so had but little time to harvest their ill-gotten gains. Even Julius Caesar, when he was Governor of Spain in 61 B.C., made a fortune large enough to pay off all his huge debts in Rome. Cicero, on the other hand, amazed the people of Cilicia in Asia Minor when he showed himself an honest and mild ruler. Of course, if a provincial governor overstepped the wide limits that practice allowed, he might be put on trial in Rome when he returned, as was Verres, the ruffianly governor of Sicily in 71 B.C. But juries might be bribed unless the case was too bad to cover up, and the governors of provinces were seldom brought to book.

With the Empire, however, began a better time for the provinces. One of the greatest services that Augustus and his successors rendered to the world was that they gave good government to the provinces.

XX

THE ROMAN LAW-COURTS

In the earliest times the seat of justice in Rome was the Tribunal. This was a raised platform at one end of the Forum itself, where the praetor used to sit in his chair of state to hear both sides of any legal question in dispute between citizens. Round the platform there were seats for those interested in the case. This open-air court was quite typical of Rome, but long before the time of Caesar and Cicero the praetors had to have more suitable courts in which to hear cases. Hence in the last century B.C. justice was administered at Rome in the great basilicae near the Forum.

There were two praetors in the civil courts. One dealt with disputes between Roman citizens. The other dealt with cases in which foreigners were concerned. These two praetors had nothing to do with the trial of criminals. Their duty was to settle disputes between one citizen (*civis*) and another; so we say that they dealt with civil cases—disputes over land and contracts, and similar matters. In simple cases the praetor, after hearing both sides, was able to give his decision immediately. But in cases that involved knotty points of law he appointed an umpire (*arbiter*), summoned both parties to appear before him, and set forth the points of law involved. When the umpire gave his verdict the praetor had to carry it into effect.

When for any reason a case had to be put off to another day, the man who had brought the action into court called upon his opponent to give bail—i.e. to pay down a sum of money himself or find a friend who would do so, as a guarantee that he would appear in court at the next hearing.

If either of the two parties without good reason failed to put in an appearance when the case was resumed, the verdict was given against him.

Let us now turn to criminal trials. The method changed very much between the time of the kings and the end of the Republic. The kings had the right to try and to punish criminals themselves, on the same grounds as a parent has the right to punish his children. When the kings were expelled, the consuls took over this duty. But the pride of the Romans even at an early date led to the arrangement that a criminal might be tried only by his fellow citizens in one of their assemblies. A magistrate always acted as accuser; the evidence was heard by the whole body of citizens; and the final verdict was passed by the assembly in the same way as a law. (In this we are reminded of impeachments in English history, when the House of Commons acted as accusers, the Lords were the judges, and the verdict was set forth in an Act of Parliament.) This method of trial by the citizen assemblies was very inconvenient, and became more so as the number of citizens increased. Accordingly, in the last century of the Republic, a new method was adopted.

Courts were created to deal with different classes of crimes —e. g. one with treason, another with forgery, a third with murder, and so on. A *praetor* was appointed to preside in each court, and he had the assistance of a body of jurors, called *iudices*. There were six *praetors* to judge criminal trials, and, as they were appointed by the people as a whole in their assembly, their decision in all cases was final.

Let us now follow the stages of a trial. The jury was sworn in, and the case began. The facts were laid before the jury, sometimes in the form of documents, sometimes as spoken evidence of witnesses who had taken an oath to speak

THE TARPEIAN ROCK ON THE CAPITOL

as it is to-day

truthfully. The accused was allowed to bring in his friends to speak in his favour. They were called *laudatores* and might be anything up to ten in number. Slaves only gave evidence under torture, so what they had to say about a crime was always read out in court, having been written down beforehand. When all the evidence had been heard, the jury considered their verdict. Each man wrote down his judgement on a wax tablet and put it in an urn. The verdict of each juror was expressed by one of three letters: A, for *absolvo*, standing for Not Guilty; C, for *condemno*, standing for Guilty; and N.L., for *non liquet*, standing for Not Proven, as they say in the Scottish courts when the matter is open to doubt. The tablets were taken from the urn and the verdict was decided by the majority of votes. If the jury could not decide to condemn or acquit the accused, the judge announced the fact by the one word *Amplius*, meaning that the matter must be reconsidered more fully when more evidence had been obtained.

If the accused was guilty, the chances were that his punishment would not be particularly severe. This was partly because of the honourable position enjoyed by a Roman citizen—*civis Romanus sum* was a proud boast and one that carried great privileges for those who could claim it; or the accused might altogether escape punishment from the fact that he was not necessarily in court and might be able to make good his escape as soon as the verdict was announced. A Roman awaiting trial was not imprisoned; at the most he might be put in charge of one of the higher magistrates. Nor was he taken forcibly to court to be tried; we may remember how Cicero led by the hand into the Senate House a man who was a proved traitor at the time of Catiline's conspiracy. Paul made known his Roman citizenship, it will be remembered, when he was imprisoned at Philippi, and his gaoler, afraid of the consequence of keeping a Roman in bonds, was anxious for him to be gone and to make no complaint.

Only for very serious crimes did a Roman forfeit his life, and then it might be by hanging, beheading, strangulation, or by being cast down from the Tarpeian Rock. For other offences a Roman might be exiled. He might go of his own free will to avoid more serious punishment; or he might be obliged to flee by being denied 'fire and water', the necessary things of life, if he remained on Italian soil. He might lose his freedom by being sold as a slave as the punishment for military offences, or for avoiding taxation, or for debt; but he was seldom, if ever, imprisoned, though the Senate might imprison a man if his liberty was thought to be dangerous to the State. The punishment might be a fine. If none of these was suitable there still remained what was known as *infamia*, by which a Roman lost some of his right of citizenship, especially the vote and often social rank. These were the ordinary punishments. They were not unduly harsh, and they were meted out after a trial that was in the main fair and just, though unfortunately money could easily be used to buy a verdict.

XXI

OUR DEBT TO ROME

ROME continued the greatest power in the world for a longer period than any other nation before or since. More than six centuries separate the humbling of Carthage in 204 B.C. from the overthrow of the Empire by the barbarians in the 5th century A.D. Compared with Rome, the British Empire is a mere baby—she has stood so far for only 150 years. France and Spain were the leading powers for less than a century each. In the ancient world, Athens rose to greatness and then declined in less than one hundred years, and the Jews were a great nation for two generations only. Yet for twenty generations Rome was supreme—a period as long as that which separates us from the battle of Crécy. Small wonder, then, that even the barbarians who overthrew the Empire believed that Rome must remain for ever the centre of the world, while even to-day, after half a dozen later empires have risen and declined, we still call Rome the 'Eternal City'.

Necessarily Rome made a deep impression on the ways and minds of men. In this brief survey of everyday life in ancient Rome we have frequently noticed that Roman customs still survive in many departments of life, and especially in those countries, like France, that were under the direct and close influence of Rome for several centuries. But apart from innumerable customs and practices, Rome bequeathed to the world a great legacy from which we still draw benefits.

First of all we owe a debt to Rome for preserving and passing on to us the glories of earlier civilizations, especially that of Greece. Though the Romans went as conquerors they fell under the spell of Greece, and in many ways adopted Greek ideas. In this fashion these ideas were handed on to us, so that we owe to Rome a large part of our debt to Greece.

Secondly, the spread of Christianity was considerably helped by Rome. The new faith was founded just as the Empire was reaching its greatest extent. True it was at first an obscure and despised religion, practised in secret: but even so it spread slowly through the Roman world. Then came the recognition of Christianity—it became the official religion of the Empire and spread like fire to the farthest outposts, aided and quickened by the world-wide government that had adopted it. When the Empire was broken to pieces, the Christian religion survived to remind men of the universal rule of the Caesars. The Popes took the place of the Emperors, and the Church remained, in the words of Hobbes, 'the ghost of the Roman Empire seated on the ruins thereof'.

Next we find that a large part of the civilized world of to-day derives its legal systems directly from the Romans. Their laws were hard but they were very just, and after the confusion caused by the barbarian conquests men turned with relief to the ordered impartial laws which were the basis of the *Pax Romana*. England, never more than an outpost of the Empire and never really colonized, is one of the very few countries that have not borrowed largely from the Roman legal system.

Again, there is the debt of the world to Roman engineering. The more this is studied the more striking is the fact that practically all of our modern engineering methods have been copied or developed from Roman models. To take a single instance—the Romans greatly excelled in bridge-building, and they were particularly successful in grounding the piers of their bridges under water. A study of Vitruvius, the great Roman authority on this subject, shows that there is scarcely a method in use to-day that has not its counterpart, usually a very close one, in Roman methods. These bridges that the Romans made seem to have been built to last till the end of time. In several countries where the Romans held sway, and particularly in France and Spain, there remain magnificent specimens of their bridges, some of them still in use after two thousand years. The Roman roads are perhaps better known in this country as an example of the Romans' skill in engineering. The whole Empire was covered, as we have seen, with a network of broad straight roads, all leading to Rome, for the use of armies, traders, couriers, and government officials. For the greater part of the Middle Ages they remained the only roads of any account; and to this day the traveller will often chance upon a stretch of perfectly straight road along which the legions had marched.

Lastly there is the debt of language. All over Southern Europe the Romans planted their colonies and quartered their troops. In those countries, such as France and Spain, where the contact of conqueror and conquered was close and intimate, the tribal tongues were forgotten in the universal use of Latin. Local and historical reasons have brought changes into these different languages, but they remain close to their common prototype, and are all known as the 'Romance' languages to remind us of their source. In one country at least, Rumania, it is a matter of national pride for the people to look back to a Roman origin for their language. A further advantage followed from the universal use of Latin. It remained the language of all educated men throughout the Middle Ages. Intercourse was therefore much easier than when there is a language barrier; and though ideas stagnated somewhat during the Middle Ages, when the revival of learning came in the fifteenth century the wealth of new ideas could be shared by all educated men since they could express their thoughts in a language known to all, that is, in Latin.

We speak of Latin as a 'dead' language since it is not used as the everyday speech of any nation; but despite this there is every reason why it should be regarded as a most profitable study. Even an elementary knowledge of the subject will make us better and keener students of our own wonderful language, since the proportion of English words derived directly from the Latin, or indirectly through the 'Romance' languages, is a high one. True there has been a tendency since the middle of last century to get back to words of Saxon origin; and this tendency we cannot but applaud. In recent years, with the advance of science and modern discovery,

A ROMAN ROAD
The Appian Way leading south from Rome (see map, p. 14)

there has been the practice of going to the 'dead' languages (Latin and Greek) for the new vocabulary required.

Further, the study of a highly inflected language like Latin is valuable for English boys and girls whose mother tongue is almost without inflexions. Moreover, a grasp of Latin calls for clear thinking, and the study of it is a valuable form of mental exercise that helps the student towards a ready understanding of intellectual problems in general. Indeed, Matthew Arnold used to hold that no man might claim to be truly educated without a knowledge of the classics, and it has been proved again and again that a person brought up in the classical tradition can turn his hand readily to very different mental tasks.

APPENDIX I

Abbreviations of *Praenomina* (see Chap. vi, p. 56):

A.	Aulus.	L.	Lucius.	S.	Sextus.
App.	Appius.	M.	Marcus.	Ser.	Servius.
C.	Gaius.	M'.	Manius.	Sp.	Spurius.
Cn.	Gnaeus.	P.	Publius.	T.	Titus.
D.	Decimus.	Q.	Quintus.	Ti.	Tiberius.

Other common abbreviations:

A.U.C. (in dates)=*Ab Urbe Condita*: i. e. 'from the founding of the City' (753 B.C.).

HS.=*Sestertius*.

Imp.=*Imperator* (similarly, Leg.=*Legatus*; Pr.=*Praetor*; Q.= *Quaestor*; &c.).

P.C.=*Patres Conscripti*, the title of the assembled Senate.

P.M.=*Pontifex Maximus*.

S.=*Salutem*
S.P.D.=*Salutem plurimam dicit* }(formulae for beginning a letter).

S.P.Q.R.=*Senatus Populusque Romanus* (the inscription found on the standards of the legions).

S.C.=*Senatus Consultum*; a decree of the Senate. These letters are found on all coins struck by command of the Senate.

Abbreviations of Latin words in use to-day:

a.m. =*ante meridiem* (before noon).

p.m.=*post meridiem* (after noon).

cf. =*confer*, compare.

e.g. =*exempli gratia*, for example.

etc. =*et cetera*, and the rest.

ibid.=*ibidem*, in the same place.

id. =*idem*, the same.

i.e. =*id est*, that is.

l.c. or loc. cit.=*loco citato*, in the place mentioned.

N.B.=*nota bene*, note specially.

P.S. =*postscriptum*, something written afterwards.

q.v. =*quod vide*, which see.

sc. =*scilicet*, namely.

viz. =*videlicet*, namely.

v. =*versus*, against.

APPENDIX II

MARCH	1st	Kalendae	Kal. Mart.
	2nd		a.d. vi Non. Mart.
	3rd		a.d. v Non. Mart.
	4th		a.d. iv Non. Mart.
	5th		a.d. iii Non. Mart.
	6th		Pr. Non. Mart.
	7th	Nonae	Non. Mart.
	8th		a.d. viii Id. Mart.
	9th		a.d. vii Id. Mart.
	10th		a.d. vi Id. Mart.
	11th		a.d. v Id. Mart.
	12th		a.d. iv Id. Mart.
	13th		a.d. iii Id. Mart.
	14th		Pr. Id. Mart.
	15th	Idus	Id. Mart.
	16th		a.d. xvii Kal. Apr.
	17th		a.d. xvi Kal. Apr.
	18th		a.d. xv Kal. Apr.
	19th		a.d. xiv Kal. Apr.
	20th		a.d. xiii Kal. Apr.
	21st		a.d. xii Kal. Apr.
	22nd		a.d. xi Kal. Apr.
	23rd		a.d. x Kal. Apr.
	24th		a.d. ix Kal. Apr.
	25th		a.d. viii Kal. Apr.
	26th		a.d. vii Kal. Apr.
	27th		a.d. vi Kal. Apr.
	28th		a.d. v Kal. Apr.
	29th		a.d. iv Kal. Apr.
	30th		a.d. iii Kal. Apr.
	31st		Pr. Kal. Apr.

The Roman method of reckoning the days of the month is set out fully in Chap. xii, on p. 99. To illustrate this in a specimen month, the calendar for March is here printed in full. In the second column are found the three chief days in the month, from which the other days were reckoned. It will be noticed that in March the Nones and the Ides fall irregularly on the 7th and 15th instead of on the 5th and 13th.

INDEX

(Mainly of Latin terms)

PRINTED IN GREAT BRITAIN AT THE UNIVERSITY PRESS, OXFORD
BY VIVIAN RIDLER, PRINTER TO THE UNIVERSITY